A DICKENS CHRONOLOGY

D0989643

A Dickens Chronology

NORMAN PAGE

G.K.HALL&CO.

70 LINCOLN STREET, BOSTON, MASS.

© Norman Page 1988

Published 1988 in the United States of America and Canada by
G. K. HALL & CO.
70 Lincoln Street
Boston, Massachusetts 02111

First published 1988 by
THE MACMILLAN PRESS LTD
Houndmills, Basingstoke
Hampshire RG21 2XS

Printed in Hong Kong

Library of Congress Cataloging-in-Publication Data
Page, Norman.
A Dickens chronology.
Bibliography: p.
Includes index.
1. Dickens, Charles, 1812–1870—Chronology.
I. Title.
PR4587.P34   1988   823'.8   87–25209
ISBN 0–8161–8949–8

Contents

Contents

General Editor's Preface

Most biographies are ill adapted to serve as works of reference – not surprisingly so, since the biographer is likely to regard his function as the devising of a continuous and readable narrative, with excursions into interpretation and speculation, rather than a bald recital of facts. There are times, however, when anyone reading for business or pleasure needs to check a point quickly or to obtain a rapid overview of part of an author's life or career; and at such moments turning over the pages of a biography can be a time-consuming and frustrating occupation. The present series of volumes aims at providing a means whereby the chronological facts of an author's life and career, rather than needing to be prised out of the narrative in which they are (if they appear at all) securely embedded, can be seen at a glance. Moreover, whereas biographies are often, and quite understandably, vague over matters of fact (since it makes for tediousness to be forever enumerating details of dates and places), a chronology can be precise whenever it is possible to be precise.

Thanks to the survival, sometimes in very large quantities, of letters, diaries, notebooks and other documents, as well as to thoroughly researched biographies and bibliographies, this material now exists in abundance for many major authors. In the case of, for example, Dickens, we can often ascertain what he was doing in each month and week, and almost on each day, of his prodigiously active working life; and the student of, say, *David Copperfield* is likely to find it fascinating as well as useful to know just when Dickens was at work on each part of that novel, what other literary enterprises he was engaged in at the same time, whom he was meeting, what places he was visiting, and what were the relevant circumstances of his personal and professional life. Such a chronology is not, of course, a substitute for a biography; but its arrangement, in combination with its index, makes it a much more convenient tool for this kind of purpose; and it may be acceptable as a form of 'alternative' biography, with its own distinctive advantages as well as its obvious limitations.

Since information relating to an author's early years is usually scanty and chronologically imprecise, the opening section of some volumes in this series groups together the years of childhood and adolescence. Thereafter each year, and usually each month, is dealt with separately. Information not readily assignable to a specific month or day is given as a general note under the relevant year or month. The first entry for each month carries an indication of the day of the week, so that when necessary this can be readily calculated for other dates. Each volume also contains a bibliography of the principal sources of information. In the chronology itself, the sources of many of the more specific items, including quotations, are identified, in order that the reader who wishes to do so may consult the original contexts.

NORMAN PAGE

Introduction

Despite some regrettable gaps in the record, most obviously those relating to the childhood years and the relationship with Ellen Ternan, Dickens's life is richly documented. As a result, a chronology that is not to become impossibly bloated must be highly selective; and, since any selection involves the continual exercise of personal judgement, the reader or reviewer who finds pleasure in noting omissions will suffer no shortage of employment in perusing this volume. Little has been included to which a definite date cannot be assigned with reasonable confidence, and much has been omitted that is known but has seemed to me too trivial to be worth including or that, if included, might have obscured the main outlines of what is presented. In the first of these respects at least, that of factual exactness, this *Chronology* may be superior to some biographies cast in more conventional forms. Besides deploying its information more accessibly than the latter usually do, it tries to avoid the vague or cavalier approach to chronological accuracy that even the best of them sometimes betray. Of course, a biographer's proper business is not limited to the presentation of facts; but one does not need to be a Gradgrind to insist that the facts, and their accuracy, are of primary importance if biography is to be a branch of history rather than a sub-genre of fiction.

Consider, for example, the case of the student or reader who, knowing of Dickens's famous quarrel and no less famous reconciliation with Thackeray, wishes to learn as quickly and precisely as possible when that reconciliation took place. At the outset, a good deal of to-and-froing between index and text is usually necessary before the relevant passages can be located – assuming, that is, that the required standard works lie conveniently to hand. But that is only the beginning of the enquirer's troubles. Some sources are of no help at all: Forster's biography of Dickens, for example, refers to the episode dismissively (and unconvincingly) as 'hardly now worth mention even in a note' – Forster being evidently concerned to play down this passage in his hero's relationships. J. W. T. Ley, Forster's twentieth-century editor, does consider it worth a note and tells us, with what sounds like confident precision, that the reconciliation occurred 'only three weeks before' Thackeray's death on Christmas Eve 1863. Edgar

Johnson, Dickens's most important modern biographer, places the event more vaguely 'a few weeks before Thackeray's death' – this on p. 936 of his book, though by p. 1014 the interval has unaccountably shrunk to 'only the week before'. Michael and Mollie Hardwick in their *Charles Dickens Encyclopaedia* give the interval as 'a week'; Leslie Stephen in the *Dictionary of National Biography* gives it as 'a few days'; Norman and Jeanne MacKenzie in their recent biography of Dickens are cautiously vague, or perhaps simply evasive ('just before his last illness'). Some of Thackeray's biographers are no more helpful: Lionel Stevenson locates the reconciliation in the last week of Thackeray's life, while Malcolm Elwin altogether avoids the question of a date. One of them, however, settles the matter and in the process demonstrates the unreliability of the rest: Gordon Ray in his *Thackeray: The Age of Wisdom* tells us that the two novelists renewed their friendship 'probably sometime in early May [1863]' – that is, between seven and eight months before Thackeray's death; and, since Professor Ray's statement is based on what is apparently the only surviving contemporary account, the unpublished diary of Henry Silver, it can be accepted as the nearest to the truth that we are likely to attain.

As this small-scale example suggests, even distinguished and normally dependable biographers occasionally nod, and there are obvious dangers for the seeker after truth who consults just one such authority and takes its statements on trust. These lapses may occur because the writers are momentarily swept off their feet by the drama of the unfolding life-story: after all, it makes a much more telling narrative point to have the reconciliation taking place more or less on Thackeray's deathbed. Sometimes the facts have their own drama – Dickens's reconciliation with another erstwhile friend, Mark Lemon, really does seem to have taken place at a graveside – but in no circumstances should they have a spurious drama foisted upon them, and it seems worth trying to get right such facts as are capable of being got right.

Not that a chronological recital such as that which follows can be wholly objective, of course: as Julian Barnes has demonstrated in *Flaubert's Parrot*, chronologies can have their own axes to grind, and inclusion, omission and juxtaposition can enforce or undermine a particular interpretation of the facts. With few exceptions, I have tried to avoid the grosser varieties of interpretation and surmise, and have confined myself to what is ascertainable. It will be surprising, however, not to say miraculous, if errors have not crept into this book, and I shall be grateful to have them, along with any inexcusable omissions, pointed out.

The varying density of coverage in different parts of the chronology often reflects the relative interest of, and abundance of materials available for, different phases of Dickens's life: his first American tour, for example, was a period of intense activity that is documented with unusual fullness. Like the brick-maker, however, the chronologist is at the mercy of his materials, and there are some regrettable hiatuses – though some of these may carry their own message, as with the sparse records of some of Dickens's later years when his secret liaison with Ellen Ternan was presumably absorbing much of his time, but from which no correspondence between the two lovers has come to light.

This book is designed as a reference tool, and not many readers will care to go through it from beginning to end; but even to study the entries for a year or two may offer not only a good deal of precise information but a strong impression of Dickens's life as it was lived: the living, it goes without saying, including the work that gives the life the greatest part of its interest.

Quotations from Dickens's letters are identified by the name of the recipient and the date (where the latter differs from that of the entry in question). A note on the principal sources consulted will be found at the end of the chronology. Extracts from *The Pilgrim Edition of the Letters of Charles Dickens*, volumes I–V, have been quoted by kind permission of Oxford University Press. I owe a more personal, and very substantial, debt to Professor Philip Collins, who kindly suggested numerous improvements and also gave me access to his unpublished lists of Dickens's readings, thus enabling me to supplement the evidence from other sources with much additional information on this important topic, and to his file on the *Gad's Hill Gazette*, which supplied several further items relating to Dickens's social life in 1864–6.

List of Abbreviations

The abbreviation CD throughout refers to Charles Dickens, and JF to John Forster. The following abbreviations are used for Dickens's writings and for the magazines with which he was involved.

AN	*American Notes*
AYR	*All the Year Round*
BR	*Barnaby Rudge*
CC	*A Christmas Carol*
D&S	*Dombey and Son*
DC	*David Copperfield*
ED	*Edwin Drood*
GE	*Great Expectations*
HT	*Hard Times*
HW	*Household Words*
LD	*Little Dorrit*
MC	*Martin Chuzzlewit*
MHC	*Master Humphrey's Clock*
NN	*Nicholas Nickleby*
OCS	*The Old Curiosity Shop*
OMF	*Our Mutual Friend*
OT	*Oliver Twist*
PP	*The Pickwick Papers*
SB	*Sketches by Boz*
TTC	*A Tale of Two Cities*
UT	*The Uncommercial Traveller*

The Dickens Family

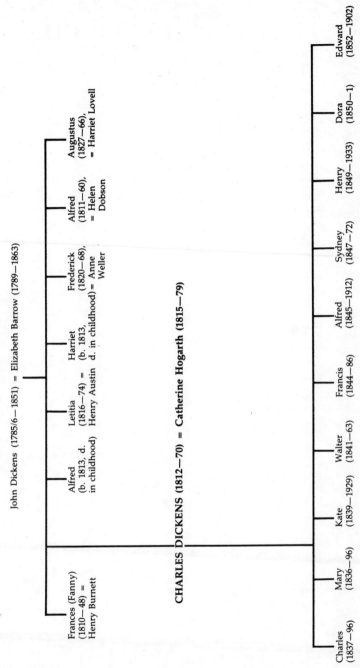

John Dickens (1785/6—1851) = Elizabeth Barrow (1789—1863)

Frances (Fanny)
(1810—48) =
Henry Burnett

Alfred
(b. 1813, d.
in childhood)

Letitia
(1816—74) =
Henry Austin

Harriet
(b. 1813,
d. in childhood)

Frederick
(1820—68) = Anne
Weller

Alfred
(1811—60),
= Helen
Dobson

Augustus
(1827—66),
= Harriet Lovell

CHARLES DICKENS (1812—70) = Catherine Hogarth (1815—79)

Charles
(1837—96)

Mary
(1836—96)

Kate
(1839—1929)

Walter
(1841—63)

Francis
(1844—86)

Alfred
(1845—1912)

Sydney
(1847—72)

Henry
(1849—1933)

Dora
(1850—1)

Edward
(1852—1902)

The Dickens Family

A Dickens Chronology

1812

7 February (Fri)   Charles John Huffam Dickens is born at 13 Mile End Terrace, Landport, Portsmouth (now 396 Commercial Road and the Dickens Birthplace Museum), the second child of John Dickens (1785/6–1851), a clerk in the Navy Pay Office, and Elizabeth Dickens, née Barrow (1789–1863), who had married at St Mary-le-Strand, London, on 13 June 1809. Their first child, Frances (Fanny), had been born on 28 October 1810. The boy is named Charles after his maternal grandfather; John after his father; Huffam (misspelt Huffham in the baptismal register) after his godfather, Christopher Huffam, a prosperous naval rigger of 5 Church Row, Limehouse.

4 March   The child is baptised at St Mary's, Kingston, Portsea. (The church was demolished in the 1850s, but the font is now in St Stephen's, Portsea.)

?24 June   The Dickens family move, possibly to lodgings at 16 Hawke Street, Portsmouth (destroyed in the Second World War).

1813

December   The Dickens family move again, to 39 Wish Street (now Kings Road), Southsea (now demolished).

1814

28 March   Birth of Alfred Allen Dickens, brother of CD.

6 September   Death of Alfred Dickens, 'of water on the brain' according to an announcement in the local newspaper.

1815

?January   The Dickens family move to lodgings in London, possibly at 10 Norfolk Street (now 22 Cleveland Street), John Dickens having been transferred to duties at Somerset House apparently with effect from 1 January.

1816

23 April   Birth of Letitia Mary Dickens, sister of CD.

1817

?January   John Dickens is moved again, possibly to Sheerness, Kent for a short period, then to Chatham, Kent, where the family settle at 2 (now 11) Ordnance Terrace (still standing, under private ownership). Their neighbours at no. 1 are the Stroughill family, and CD later becomes friendly with George and Lucy Stroughill.

1819

?August   Birth of Harriet Ellen Dickens, sister of CD; she is baptised on 3 September and dies in infancy (date unknown but before the move to London in 1822).

14 August   John Dickens borrows £200 from James Milbourne.

1820

July   Birth of Frederick William Dickens, brother of CD (baptised on 4 Aug).

1821

Summer   The Dickens family move to a smaller house at 18 St Mary's Place (also known as The Brook), Chatham (now demolished). CD, who has had his first lessons from his mother and has later attended a dame's school in Rome Lane (see 'Our School', *HW*, 11 Oct 1851, also in *Reprinted Pieces*), is now sent to a school kept by William Giles, son of the minister of the Baptist chapel next to the Dickens home.

11 December Mary Allen (Mrs Thomas Allen, née Barrow, widowed maternal aunt of CD known as Aunt Fanny), who has lived with the Dickens family for most of CD's life up to this point, marries Dr Matthew Lamert and moves to Ireland. Before this time Dr Lamert, an army surgeon, has frequently taken CD, together with his own son James, to the Theatre Royal, Chatham, and to other theatrical performances; and this custom is continued by James Lamert after the departure of his father and step-mother.

1822

11 March Birth of Alfred Lamert Dickens, brother of CD.

?June John Dickens is transferred back to Somerset House, with a reduction in income from £440 to £350 per annum. CD may have stayed behind in Chatham with Mr Giles for a short time before rejoining his family, who settle at 16 Bayham Street, Camden Town (now demolished).

September Death of Mary Lamert, aunt of CD, in Ireland.

After the return to London, John Dickens's debts become more pressing, and CD is not sent to school.

1823

9 April Fanny Dickens becomes a pupil at the Royal Academy of Music and remains there until midsummer 1827.

Towards the end of this year – perhaps at Michaelmas (29 Sept) – the Dickens family move to 4 Gower Street North (demolished 1895), where CD's mother attempts unsuccessfully to start a school.

1824

Early in the year (date uncertain, but perhaps 9 Feb), CD is sent to work at Warren's blacking-warehouse at Hungerford Stairs, Strand (now demolished, the site being occupied by Victoria Embankment Gardens). Before the end of his time there, the business moves to Chandos Street, Covent Garden.

20 February   John Dickens is arrested for debt at the suit of James Karr, cobbler, and is conveyed to the Marshalsea Prison in Borough High Street. Probably in late March or early April, the Gower Street house is given up, Mrs Dickens and three of her children move into the prison, and CD is placed in lodgings with a family friend, Mrs Roylance, in Little College Street, Camden Town (house now demolished; street now known as College Place). After a few weeks, he moves into an attic in Lant Street, Southwark, near the prison, and is able to have breakfasts and suppers with his family. Meanwhile, on 2 March, John Dickens has applied for retirement from the Navy Pay Office on medical grounds. At about this time Christopher Huffam goes bankrupt.

26 April   Death of Elizabeth Dickens, CD's paternal grandmother. John Dickens later inherits £450 (will proved 4 June) but touches none of the money, which goes to his creditors.

28 May   John Dickens is released from prison under the Insolvent Debtors' Act – that is, by coming to an arrangement with his creditors and not, as often stated, as a result of the above legacy. (He submitted his petition on 4 May and it was heard on the 27th.) According to JF, the Dickens family live for a time with Mrs Roylance, then move to a house in Hampstead. Later in the year (date uncertain, but perhaps Midsummer), they move again, to 29 Johnson Street (now Cranleigh Street), Somers Town.

The length of CD's employment at the blacking-warehouse is uncertain. The autobiographical fragment states, 'I have no idea how long it lasted; whether for a year, or much more, or less'; but Langton (*The Childhood and Youth of CD*, p. 79) points out that 'the probability is that little Charles Dickens was employed at the blacking warehouse for less than one year, and that he left it somewhere in the summer of 1824'; and Ley states that the period 'could hardly have lasted longer than six months' (JF, *Life*, ed. Ley, p. 37). Johnson dates the beginning of CD's employment 'on a Monday morning only two days after his twelfth birthday' – that is,

9 February 1824 – and states that the period spent there was 'little over four months, five at most' (*CD: His Tragedy and Triumph*, p. 45). After a quarrel with James Lamert, John Dickens withdrew his son from Warren's and (in June according to Langton, Wright, Johnson, and others), sent him to Wellington House Academy in Granby Street, Hampstead Road (now demolished), where he remained for between two and three years.

1825

9 March   John Dickens retires from the Navy Pay Office on a pension of £145 per annum, and thereafter supplements his income by occasional journalism.

27 September   The Stockton and Darlington railway is opened for passengers.

1827

?March   CD leaves Wellington House Academy, completing his formal education, of which he later writes, 'I had begun an irregular rambling education under a clergyman [Mr Giles] at Chatham, and I finished it at a good school in London – tolerably early, for my father was not a rich man, and I had to begin the world' (to J. H. Kuenzel, ?July 1838). At about this time, the Dickens family are evicted from Johnson Street for non-payment of rent, and move into lodgings at 17 The Polygon, Somers Town (now demolished). In March, CD is engaged as a clerk by Charles Molloy, solicitor, of 6 Symonds Inn, Chancery Lane. After a few weeks, he moves to another firm of solicitors, Ellis and Blackmore, of 5 Holborn Court, Gray's Inn (now 1 South Square), at a wage of 10s. a week, later rising to 15s. Shortly afterwards, the firm moves to 1 Raymond Buildings. During this period CD frequents the London theatres and also learns Gurney's system of shorthand, 'that savage stenographic mystery' (*DC*, ch. 43).

November   Birth of Augustus Newnham Dickens, youngest brother of CD, later nicknamed Moses.

1828

November CD leaves Ellis & Blackmore and begins work as a freelance shorthand reporter at Doctors' Commons. He lives with his parents, who by now have moved to lodgings over a shop in Norfolk Street (see next entry).

1830–1

8 February On the day after his 18th birthday, CD obtains a reader's ticket for the British Museum, giving his address as 10 Norfolk Street, Fitzroy Square (now 22 Cleveland Street).

?May CD meets Maria Beadnell, daughter of George Beadnell (died 1862), who is employed by Smith, Payne and Smith's bank in Lombard Street, where the Beadnells live next to the bank. A little later, CD falls in love with Maria and his infatuation continues for three or four years. The chronology relating to Maria Beadnell is uncertain. Most accounts state that her parents, aware of CD's feelings for their daughter and unimpressed by the young man's prospects (and his father's insolvency), sent her to Paris to get her out of CD's way; that she was at finishing-school there in 1831–2; and that she returned 'strangely altered' and decidedly cool in her attitude towards him. But Michael Slater has persuasively argued (*Dickens and Women*, pp. 51–2) that, since it is now known that Maria was in Paris in April 1830, it is more likedly that CD 'declared himself to her and perhaps received some encouragement' in May 1830, *after* her sojourn in Paris. Towards the end of 1831, CD attends a dinner-party given by the Beadnells for which he writes a set of facetious verses, 'The Bill of Fare', in which he refers to having 'lost his [heart] a twelve month ago, from last May' – that is, in or about May 1830.

1832

Early in the year, CD joins the staff of *The Mirror of Parliament*, started in 1828 by his uncle, John Henry Barrow, as a rival to *Hansard*. He is employed (as his father also is) in taking down proceedings in the House of Commons. He moves to lodgings in

Cecil Street, Strand, for a time, but soon returns to the parental home. At about the same time he also becomes a parliamentary reporter on an evening newspaper, *The True Sun* (published from 5 Mar 1832 and edited by Samuel Blanchard), but remains there for only a few months. (The chronology of these events is, again, uncertain. Johnson states, 'It is not clear which engagement preceded the other, but for a time he certainly worked concurrently on both publications' – *CD: His Tragedy and Triumph*, p. 61. Forster states unequivocally that 'his first parliamentary service was given to the *True Sun*', and that he 'was nineteen years old when at last he entered the gallery' [i.e. before 7 Feb 1832]; but this dating seems to be incorrect. CD himself said [20 May 1865], 'I went into the gallery of the House of Commons as a Parliamentary reporter when I was a boy not eighteen', but his memory must have been faulty.) Among much else, he reports the debates leading to the abolition of slavery in 1833 and speeches by Daniel O'Connell, and probably reports Gladstone's maiden speech on 3 June 1833. He applies for an audition at Covent Garden Theatre, with a view to becoming a professional actor, but is prevented from attending by a cold and never renews his application.

7 August   The reformed parliament meets for the first time.

1833

7 February   CD's twenty-first birthday. His parents are by now living at 18 Bentinck Street, Manchester Square, having apparently moved there early in January. His birthday-party on the 11th is attended by Beard, Kolle, and others.

18 March   Discouraged by her 'displays of heartless indifference', CD breaks off his relationship with Maria Beadnell and returns her letters. (See also 9 Feb 1855.)

21 May   CD is best man at the wedding of his friend Henry Kolle and Anne Beadnell, sister of Maria.

June   CD asks Richard Earle to recommend him as a 'Short Hand Writer' if the opportunity arises.

27 July   Dines with John Payne Collier, reporter for the *Morning Chronicle*.

1 December   'A Dinner at Poplar Walk', CD's first published sketch, appears anonymously in the *Monthly Magazine* (see the Preface to the 1847 edn of *PP*).

During this year, CD's operatic burlesque *O'Thello* is privately performed by his family and friends.

1834

During this year, CD publishes six more sketches in the *Monthly Magazine*. In August he uses the pseudonym 'Boz' for the first time.

August   CD becomes a reporter on the *Morning Chronicle* at 5 (soon rising to 7) guineas a week.

September   Visits Edinburgh with Beard to report on a banquet given to Lord Grey; their report appears in the *Morning Chronicle* on the 17th and 18th.

26 September–15 December   Five 'Street Sketches' are published in the *Morning Chronicle*.

?21 November   John Dickens is arrested for debt at the suit of Shaw and Maxwell, wine-merchants, and is taken to 'Sloman's in Cursitor Street', a sponging-house, where CD visits him.

December   CD moves into 13 Furnival's Inn, Holborn (now demolished), his brother Frederick sharing the chambers.

1835

31 January–20 August   Publishes twenty 'Sketches of London' in the *Evening Chronicle*, edited by John Black.

January   Goes to Essex and Suffolk to report on election nominations, and sends reports to the *Morning Chronicle* from Colchester, Braintree, Chelmsford, Sudbury and Bury St Edmunds.

1 May   In Exeter with Beard to report Lord John Russell's speech; their account is published in the *Morning Chronicle* the next day.

?May   CD becomes engaged to Catherine Hogarth, daughter of George Hogarth, journalist, music-critic, and former friend of Sir Walter Scott, of 18 York Place, Brompton. Soon afterwards, CD moves into temporary lodgings at Selwood Terrace, Brompton (probably no. 11), close to the Hogarth home, and remains there for about four months.

27 September–17 January 1836   Publishes twelve sketches in *Bell's Life in London*, edited by Vincent Dowling.

26 or 27 October   Suggests the title *Sketches by Boz* to the publisher John Macrone.

5 November   Visits Newgate and Cold Bath Fields prison to collect material for 'A Visit to Newgate' (*SB*).

7 November   Leaves for Bristol to report a speech by Russell (given on the 10th) for the *Morning Chronicle*.

1 December   In Hatfield to report on a fire at Hatfield House. Later in the month he is in Kettering to report on a by-election.

1836

February
8   (Mon) *SB* (First Series) published.
12   Chapman and Hall propose terms for *The Pickwick Papers*.
17   Moves to larger chambers at 15 Furnival's Inn.
18   'Pickwick is at length begun in all his might and glory. The first chapter, will be ready tomorrow' (to Chapman and Hall).

March
18   (Fri) The *Morning Chronicle* and *Evening Chronicle* both publish

'Our Next Door Neighbours', an 'abortive start' to a new series of *SB* (see Graham Mott, *Dickensian*, 80 [1984] 114–16).

26   *PP* advertised in *The Times*.

31   First number of *PP* appears; further monthly instalments follow to 30 October 1837.

April

2   (Sat) CD marries Catherine Hogarth in St Luke's, Chelsea. They spend a week's honeymoon at Chalk, near Gravesend, Kent.

20   Robert Seymour, illustrator of *PP*, commits suicide after completing only seven plates. R. W. Buss illustrates the third number, H. K. Browne ('Phiz') the rest of the novel.

May

9   (Mon) CD accepts Macrone's offer of £200 for 'a Work of Fiction . . . to be entitled *Gabriel Vardon, the Locksmith of London* (later retitled *Barnaby Rudge*). CD withdraws from this agreement in November after being offered £500 for the novel by Bentley.

During this month, Mrs Henry Kolle (née Anne Beadnell) dies.

June

CD publishes *Sunday under Three Heads* under the pseudonym 'Timothy Sparks'.

July

23   (Sat) CD reads his opera libretto *The Village Coquettes* to a group of friends; he sends it to John Braham on 30 July, but it is not performed until 6 December. Bentley publishes it on 22 December.

August

11   (Thurs) Accepts Thomas Tegg's offer of £100 to write 'by Christmas next' a children's book titled 'Solomon Bell the Raree Showman' (never written).

22   Signs agreement with Bentley to 'write a Novel' and to offer him 'his next novel'.

25   Accepts John Braham's offer of £30 for a two-act farce *The Strange Gentleman*, produced at the St James's Theatre on 29 September.

From late August to 24 September CD and Catherine spend a holiday of about five weeks at Petersham, near Richmond, Surrey.

November

4 (Fri) Agrees to edit *Bentley's Miscellany* from January 1837 for Richard Bentley at a salary of £20 a month. Further agreements concerning this new magazine are made on 17 March and 28 September 1837, 22 September 1838, 27 February 1839.

5 Resigns from the *Morning Chronicle*: 'I left the reputation behind me of being the best and most rapid reporter ever known' (to Wilkie Collins, 6 June 1856).

December

6 (Tues) *The Village Coquettes* is successfully produced at the St James's Theatre.

17 *SB* (Second Series) published. During this month CD is introduced to JF at Ainsworth's home, Kensal Lodge.

1837

January

6 (Fri) Birth of Charles Culliford Boz Dickens, first child of CD.

21 CD is elected a member of the Garrick Club.

31 The first instalment of *Oliver Twist* is published in *Bentley's Miscellany*, which begins publication this month; twenty-three further instalments of the novel appear irregularly to April 1839.

February

4 (Sat) CD and Catherine, accompanied by the latter's sister, Mary Hogarth, go to Chalk for a month's holiday, interrupted by frequent visits to London on business by CD. Beard visits them for a weekend (25th–27th) and they all spend a day (25th) at Chatham. They return to temporary lodgings at 30 Upper Norton Street.

This month's instalment of *PP* sells 14,000 copies; 20,000 are sold in May; 26,000 in September; 29,000 in October; and nearly 40,000 in November.

March

3 (Fri) CD's one-act burletta *Is She his Wife?* is produced at the St James's Theatre.

April
Early in the month, the Dickens family and Mary Hogarth move to 48 Doughty Street (now the Dickens House). The tenancy agreement, for three years, is dated 3 April.

May
3   (Wed) CD speaks at the Literary Fund Anniversary Dinner – his first public speech.
6   In the evening, CD, Catherine and Mary go to the St James's Theatre; soon after going to bed, Mary is suddenly taken ill.
7   Death of Mary Hogarth: she 'expired in my arms at two o'clock this afternoon' (to Edward Chapman; other letters give the time as 3 p.m.).
13   Mary is buried in Kensal Green Cemetery. Soon afterwards, CD and Catherine go to a rented cottage, Collins's Farm (now Wylde's), on the western edge of Hampstead Heath, 'for quiet and change' (to Beard, 17 May), and remain there until the beginning of June: 'I have been compelled to lay aside all thoughts of my usual monthly work' (*ibid.*), and there is no June instalment of *PP* or *OT*.

June
16   (Fri) JF introduces CD to Macready.
18   CD dines with Talfourd; among his fellow guests are JF, Macready, and Procter.
20   Accession of Queen Victoria.
26   CD goes to see Macready act and afterwards visits him in his dressing-room; JF and Browning are also among those present.
27   CD, JF, Browne, Cattermole and Macready visit Newgate and Cold Bath Fields prisons; among other prisoners at Newgate they see Thomas Wainewright, poisoner and forger; afterwards they dine at CD's home.

July
2   (Sun) CD, Catherine, and H. K. Browne go to France and Belgium for a few days.
15   CD attends the wedding of his sister Letitia to Henry Austin.

August
31   (Thurs) To Broadstairs, Kent, for a holiday with Catherine and her mother; they stay in lodgings at 12 (now 31) High Street, and CD continues work there.

September

9 (Sat) Death of Macrone. CD later edits *The Pic Nic Papers* (1841) in order to raise money for Macrone's family.

28 After a dispute with Bentley, leading to CD's resignation from the editorship of the *Miscellany*, CD signs a new agreement increasing his salary to £30 a month.

30 Goes to Covent Garden with JF, Ainsworth and Procter, to see Macready in *The Winter's Tale*.

October

31 (Tues) Goes to Brighton for a week. During this holiday CD reads Defoe's *History of the Devil*.

November

8 (Wed) CD dines at Kensal Lodge, Harrow Road, the home of Ainsworth.

18 Gives a dinner at the Prince of Wales, Leicester Square, for about fourteen guests (including Ainsworth, Browne, JF, Jerdan, Macready and Talfourd) to celebrate the completion of *PP*. Talfourd proposes CD's health and CD replies 'under strong emotion – most admirably' (Macready's diary).

29 Signs an agreement with Bentley to edit the *Memoirs of Grimaldi*.

During this month, CD opens an account at Coutts's Bank, depositing £500 of the money paid to him by Chapman and Hall out of the profits of *PP*. Serialisation of *BR* begins, continuing monthly to June 1839.

December

3 (Sun) Publishes a dramatic review in *The Examiner* (and another on the 17th).

9 Christening of Charles Culliford Boz Dickens.

12 CD dines at the home of George Cruikshank and meets J. G. Lockhart.

1838

January

2 (Tues) CD spends the day with Ainsworth; they discuss business at Macrone's office, visit the scene of a fire two days earlier in the Borough, and ascend to the top of St Saviour's

Church (now Southwark Cathedral); they dine together and then go to the Covent Garden Theatre, where they meet Browning.

3–5   CD works at the Grimaldi *Memoirs*; by the 5th he has finished all but the introduction and conclusion.

6   Charley Dickens's first birthday; among the guests at an evening party are JF, Mitton and Beard.

8   CD begins *Sketches of Young Gentlemen*.

9   Insures his life.

10   After working all day, attends an evening quadrille party at Mr Levien's and there meets Serjeant Ballantine, who later describes him as 'quite a boy' (i.e. very youthful in appearance).

13   Browne comes to dinner.

14   CD attends a demonstration of 'animal magnetism' by Dr John Elliotson at University College Hospital; later he dines at Talfourd's.

30   Sets off by coach with Browne to visit Yorkshire schools and is away until about 6 February. After spending the night of the 30th at Grantham (George Inn), they stay at the George and New Inn, Greta Bridge.

February

2   (Sat) CD and Browne call on William Shaw, principal of Bowes Academy. In a letter of 1 February to his wife, CD states that, in spite of the change of scene, he still dreams of Mary Hogarth every night; however, apparently as a result of his telling her this, the dreams thereupon cease (but see Sept 1844).

CD and Browne return to London via Darlington and York.

4   *The Examiner* publishes an enthusiastic review by CD of Macready's *King Lear*.

10   *Sketches of Young Gentlemen* published anonymously.

26   *Memoirs of Joseph Grimaldi* published.

March

6   (Tues) Birth of Mary Dickens, second child of CD.

12   Goes to see Macready in *Coriolanus*.

29   Goes to the Star and Garter, Richmond, with Catherine, who has been 'alarmingly ill' (to Bentley, 28 Mar).

31   First number of *Nicholas Nickleby* appears; eighteen further instalments run to 1 October 1839.

April

1 (Sun) JF joins CD and Catherine at Richmond, and they celebrate JF's birthday and the Dickens's wedding anniversary, which both fall on the 2nd – the first of many similar celebrations at the Star and Garter.

7 CD goes to see Macready in Byron's *The Two Foscari*.

17 Dines with JF and Browne at Greenwich.

19 Dines with Mitton.

29 Gives a dinner-party; the guests include Ainsworth, JF, Macready and Procter.

May

8 (Tues) JF and Macready dine *en famille* with CD.

12 CD speaks at a dinner of the Artists' Benevolent Fund.

29 Dines with JF and Macready.

June

During this and the next month, CD rents 4 Ailsa Park Villas, St Margaret's Road, Twickenham (still standing) as a holiday home.

21 (Thurs) Elected to the Athenaeum Club.

24 CD and Catherine dine at Elstree with the Macreadys, whose wedding-anniversary it is.

28 Coronation of Queen Victoria.

July

1 (Sun) Publishes an article, 'The Coronation', in *The Examiner*.

7 Finishes the month's number of *OT* at 11.30 p.m.

10 Begins the fifth number of *NN*.

August

10 (Fri) Signs an agreement with Henry Colburn to edit *The Pic Nic Papers* (see 9 September 1837).

September

2 (Sun) Publishes an article, 'Scott and his Publishers', in *The Examiner*.

?3 Goes to the Isle of Wight for about nine days.

22 Signs a further agreement with Bentley concerning the *Miscellany* and the publication therein of *BR* as a successor to *OT*.

October

2 (Tues) 'Nancy is no more' (to JF): that is, he has written the account of Sikes's murder of Nancy in *OT*.

13 CD and JF see Macready in *The Tempest*.

19 CD gives evidence at Bow Street Magistrates' Court in connection with the prosecution of an omnibus proprietor for cruelty to a horse, the incident having been witnessed in Carey Street on the 16th.

26 Writes a poem, 'To Ariel', in Priscilla Horton's album.

29 Sets off with Browne for a tour of the Midlands and Wales. They spend the first night at Copps' Hotel, Leamington.

30 They visit Kenilworth and Warwick castles and Stratford, where they spend the night.

31 They travel to Shrewsbury (Lion Hotel) via Birmingham and Wolverhampton; in the evening they go to the theatre in Shrewsbury.

November

1 (Thurs) CD and Browne travel to Llangollen, where they stay at the Hand Hotel.

2 At Capel Curig.

4 At Chester.

5 They are joined at Liverpool by JF, and go to Birkenhead.

6 At Manchester.

7 At Cheadle.

8 They return to London by train.

9 *OT* is published in three volumes.

21 CD goes to the Adelphi Theatre with JF to see a dramatisation of *NN* that opened on the 19th.

25 CD goes with Cruikshank to the home of Dr Elliotson (37 Conduit Street) to see a demonstration of mesmerism.

28 CD resigns from the Garrick Club; dines with Dr Elliotson.

December

5 (Wed) 'Dickens brought me his farce [*The Lamplighter*, never produced], which he read to me. . . . He reads as well as an experienced actor would – he is a surprising man' (Macready's diary).

10 Goes to Greenwich with Browne and visits Macready in the evening.

12 Takes the chair at a dinner of the Literary Fund; afterwards goes

to Covent Garden Theatre, meets Cattermole there, and sups
with him.

13 First meeting of the 'Trio Club', consisting of CD, JF and
Ainsworth, held at JF's chambers.

27 Sees JF.

28 Dines at Elliotson's.

29 Dines at Ainsworth's.

30 Dines at Talfourd's.

31 JF and Ainsworth visit CD.

1839

January

5 (Sat) Christening of Mary Dickens.

7 Party to celebrate Mary's christening and Charley's second
birthday.

12–17 CD is in Manchester with Ainsworth and JF.

22 Asks Bentley to postpone publication of *BR* in the *Miscellany* for
six months. Bentley's reply on the 25th leads CD to send him an
angry letter the next day.

28 Spends the day with Ainsworth and JF making 'new
arrangements with Bentley' (CD's diary); he decides to resign
the editorship of the *Miscellany* from 31 January (confirmed in
an agreement with Bentley dated 27 Feb), and asks Ainsworth
to take his place.

30 Ainsworth, JF, Barham, Beard and John Dickens dine at CD's
home.

February

4 (Mon) Dines at Ainsworth's; also present are JF, Barham,
Blanchard, Jerdan, Cruikshank and Leigh Hunt.

5 Dines with the Revd William Harness.

7 CD's twenty-seventh birthday: 'The end of a most prosperous
and happy year' (diary). Ainsworth, Blanchard, JF, Browne,
Mitton, CD's parents and Henry and Fanny Burnett come to
dinner.

9 Engaged in legal business; then goes to the Zoological Gardens;
reads Southey's *The Curse of Kehama*.

27 Signs an agreement with Bentley concerning *BR*.

March

4   (Mon) CD visits Exeter (staying till the 11th, at the New London Inn) to find a home for his parents, and rents for them Mile-End Cottage, Alphington (still standing), a mile from Exeter on the Plymouth Road.

13 Elected to the committee of the Royal Literary Fund.

30 Presides at a dinner of the Shakespeare Club given in Macready's honour.

April

16 (Tues) CD and JF see Macready in *King Lear*.

29 Death of Christopher Huffam, CD's godfather.

30 (until 31 Aug) Rents Elm Cottage, Petersham, for four months and spends the summer there, but with frequent visits to London for business and pleasure.

June

8   (Sat) CD, JF and Maclise attend a rehearsal of Macready's *Henry V*.

19 Dines at Sydney Smith's.

July

14 (Sun) Sends to JF 'rough notes of proposals for the New Work' (i.e. *Master Humphrey's Clock*).

16 Attends a performance of *Henry V* (see 8 June) – the last performance at Covent Garden Theatre under Macready's management.

20 Speaks at a dinner in honour of Macready.

August

7   (Wed) Visits the Macreadys at their Elstree home and is godfather at the christening of their son Henry.

21 Has been reading Scott's *Kenilworth* 'with greater delight than ever' (to Cattermole).

September

2   (Mon) CD and Catherine travel by steamer to Ramsgate; finding no lodgings there, they spend the night at the Royal Hotel and the next day go on to Broadstairs, where they begin four weeks' holiday in a rented house with 'a beautiful sea view' (CD's diary): this is 40 Albion Street, now part of the Albion Hotel. The

children join them on the same day. Samuel Rogers is also on holiday in the town.

4 '. . . thinking of the end of Nickleby' (diary). For each of the next three days the diary entry consists of the single word 'Work', which is repeated in the entries for 9–20 September inclusive.

15 Writes the preface to *NN*.

20 'Finished Nickleby this day at 2 o'clock' (diary), he sends off the final portion to the publisher at once.

21 Spends the day in London with JF, correcting proofs of the last number of *NN*; dines with JF.

22 JF goes to Broadstairs with CD and stays until the 26th.

26 Rogers calls on CD.

27 CD dines with Rogers.

29 Accompanies Rogers, who is going to France, as far as Dover.

October

1 (Tues) or 2 The Dickens family return to London from Broadstairs.

?3 'I am going forthwith tooth and nail at Barnaby' (to Cruikshank).

5 CD gives a dinner at the Albion in Aldersgate Street to celebrate the completion of *NN*, the final number of which has appeared on 30 September. The guests include Beard, Browne, Cattermole, JF, Hill, Jerdan, Maclise, Macready, Stanfield, Talfourd and Wilkie, as well as the printers and publishers. CD is presented with Maclise's portrait of him (the 'Nickleby' portrait, now in the National Portrait Gallery).

8 Dines with JF, Jerdan, Maclise and Macready.

23 *NN* published in one volume.

25 Sends presentation copy of *NN* to Macready, to whom the novel is dedicated.

29 Birth of Kate Macready Dickens.

November

19 (Tues) '. . . in the agonies of house-letting, house-taking' (to James Hall).

December

6 (Fri) CD is admitted as a student of the Middle Temple; in the event he is never called to the Bar, and petitions to withdraw on 17 March 1855.

7   Presides at a dinner of the Shakespeare Club.
Early in December, the Dickens family move to 1 Devonshire
Terrace, York Gate, Regent's Park, which remains their home until
the lease expires in 1851.
14   To CD's annoyance, Bentley advertises *BR* in the *Morning Herald*
     as 'preparing for publication'.

1840

January
1   (Wed) Gives dinner-party for Blanchard, JF, Maclise, Frank
     Stone and others.
4   Meets William Upcott.
8   'Thinking of title for new work [*MHC*] this morning' (diary).
     Dines at Chapman and Hall's.
9   Corrects proofs of *Sketches of Young Couples*; 'considering new
     work in all possible ways' (diary).
10   'I am thinking awfully, but not writing, as I intend (Please God)
     to start tomorrow' (to JF).
13   Tells Cattermole that he wishes *MHC* to be illustrated with
     'wood-cuts dropped into the text', and invites him to submit a
     sample.
14   Attends inquest (as juryman) at Marylebone Workhouse on a
     baby and is much moved by the spectacle of the young mother
     suspected of infanticide (see to JF, 15 Jan; also *Dickensian*, 70
     [1974] pp. 65–9; the experience is recalled more than twenty
     years later in 'Some Recollections of Mortality', *AYR*, 16 May
     1863, repr. in *UT*). When the case goes to the Central Criminal
     Court, where the young woman is indicted on 9 March on a
     charge of concealing the birth, CD retains a lawyer for the
     defence. The night after the inquest he is ill and sleepless.
In the latter part of this month, CD finishes the first number of
MHC, a proof of which is sent to Macready for comment on the 29th.

February
7   (Fri) CD's twenty-eighth birthday.
8   Breakfasts with Richard Monckton Milnes.
?9   '. . . confined at home with the worst cold you can conceive' (to
     T. J. Thompson).

10 *Sketches of Young Couples* is published. Wedding of Queen Victoria and Prince Albert.

11 CD tells Landor (facetiously) that he has 'fallen hopelessly in love with the Queen', and repeats the joke to other correspondents.

13 Has completed three numbers of *MHC* and the first two chapters of *BR*.

21 Bentley advertises *BR* as 'preparing for publication'.

22–5 Various newspapers print a 'contradiction' inserted by CD's solicitors, stating that 'Mr Dickens is not at present engaged upon such work' as that advertised by Bentley.

28 Sends third number of *MHC* to Chapman and Hall.

29 Travels with JF to Bath, arriving in the evening and dining with Landor.

March

4 (Wed) Returns from Bath to London.

?9 First mention of *The Old Curiosity Shop* as a title for 'that little tale' (to JF).

11 Presides at a meeting of the Literary Fund Club.

24 Calls on Macready; together they visit Maclise and JF; they dine with the latter, being joined by Blanchard, Jerdan, Procter, Stanfield and others.

During this month 'some ailments which dated from an earlier period in his life made themselves felt' (JF, *Life*) – possibly the fistula for which CD has an operation in October 1841.

April

4 (Sat) First number of *MHC* is published.

?7 'The Clock [i.e. sales of *MHC*] goes gloriously indeed' (to William Hall).

11 Calls on Maclise, and they go together to a soirée given by the Marquis of Northampton.

14 'I am very much engaged with [*MHC*]' (to L. G. Clark).

15 Declines Lady Blessington's invitation to contribute to one of her Annuals.

27 First instalment of *OCS* appears in *MHC*.

26 Thomas Beard dines at CD's home.

In the early part of the month (dates uncertain), CD spends a short time in Birmingham, and also visits Stratford and Lichfield with Catherine and JF.

May

15 (Fri) Gives a dinner-party for William Allan; Landseer and Stanfield are among the guests.

16 Second instalment of *OCS* published in *MHC*.

22-3 Attends a rehearsal of Talfourd's tragedy *Glencoe*.

23 Third instalment of *OCS* published in *MHC* (i.e. to the end of ch. 4); the remaining 69 chapters appear in 37 weekly instalments from 30 May to 6 February 1841.

June

1 (Mon) The Dickens family travel to Broadstairs, where they stay at 37 Albion Street: 'the house is beautifully situated, very clean, and very commodious' (to Thomas Mitton). On arrival, CD sets out his writing-table 'with extreme taste and neatness' (ibid.). During the month at Broadstairs, work continues on *OCS*.

10 An attempt is made on the lives of the Queen and Prince Albert in London by Edward Oxford, aged seventeen; CD tells JF soon afterwards that 'It's a great pity they couldn't suffocate that boy . . . and say no more about it.'

16 CD tells Mitton that he is 'up every morning at 7, and usually finish work for the day, before 2'.

17 Begins ch. 15 of *OCS*.

At the end of the month he is joined by JF and Maclise, and they spend two days in Chatham, Rochester and Cobham *en route* for London.

July

1 (Wed) Returns to London.

2 Agrees with Chapman and Hall that he will write *BR* for them and they will advance money for the purchase of the copyright and stock of *OT* from Bentley.

6 Attends execution of the murderer Courvoisier with Maclise and Burnett.

15 Dines with Maclise and afterwards attends a reception at Miss Coutts's.

22 Dines with Maclise; they go to the theatre afterwards.

23 Mitton dines with CD and Catherine and afterwards they all go to the Haymarket Theatre to see Macready in Bulwer's *Lady of Lyons*.

26 Complains to Landor that *OCS* demands his 'constant

attention'. In the evening CD travels by train to Basingstoke, *en route* for Devon, for a visit to his parents.

27 Arrives at Alphington: later he tells his brother Alfred that he found his parents well and comfortable.

August

4 (Tues) Returns to London from Devon.

8 Dines at Dr Elliotson's and meets Chauncy Hare Townshend.

10 Visits Townshend.

16 Macready, JF and Maclise dine at CD's home; according to Macready's diary, CD and JF quarrel, CD asks JF to leave the house, and JF apologises.

17 'I am not penitent and cannot be. . . . There is no man, alive or dead, who tries his friends as [JF] does' (to Macready).

?19 Goes to Bevis Marks in the city 'to look at a house for Sampson Brass' (to JF) – that is, as a basis for the description in *OCS*, ch. 33.

23 Macready, Maclise, JF and others dine with CD; the quarrel has evidently been patched up.

25 Christening of Kate Dickens; Macready is godfather. After the ceremony, CD, Macready and Angus Fletcher visit Cold Bath Fields Prison.

26–7 CD goes to Broadstairs to secure a holiday house.

29 'Life of "Boz"', an inaccurate biographical notice of CD, appears in *The Town*.

September

During this month, CD and his family are at Broadstairs, where work continues on *OCS*.

2 (Wed) Sends drafts of the dedication and preface to *OCS* to JF for comment.

?9 Begins ch. 38 of *OCS*, which opens the second volume; the decision that Nell must die seems to have been taken by this time.

October

2 (Fri) Sends copy for chs 44–5 of *OCS* to Chapman and Hall.

?11 Returns to London from Broadstairs.

13 Goes to Covent Garden Theatre with Macready.

15 Publication of the first volume of *MHC*.

17 Dines with Macready; Maclise and JF are also present.

20 Gives a dinner to celebrate the completion of the first volume of *MHC* to those involved with it, including 'Designers, printers, publishers, wood-cutters' (to Thomas Hill, 14 Oct).

November

2 (Mon) Works on ch. 53 of *OCS*.

3 After an unrefreshing night – 'All night I have been pursued by the child' (to JF) – CD reads ch. 53 to JF and Maclise at Jack Straw's Castle, Hampstead.

9 First performance of Edward Stirling's dramatisation of *OCS* at the Adelphi Theatre. CD does not attend, though he has been at the theatre 'all day' on the 7th and made 'a great many improvements' (to Mitton).

10 Dines with Macready.

12 Finishes the thirty-fifth number of *OCS* (i.e. to the end of ch. 55): 'The difficulty has been tremendous – the anguish unspeakable' (to JF).

17 Dines with Macready, who reads Bulwer Lytton's comedy *Money* to his guests after dinner.

24 'I am inundated with imploring letters recommending poor little Nell to mercy' (to Chapman and Hall).

25 Death of Macready's three-year-old daughter.

December

2 (Wed) Speaks at a banquet given by the Southwark Literary and Scientific Institution.

8 Attends the first performance of *Money* (see 17 Nov) at the Haymarket Theatre.

?22 Tells Cattermole that he is 'breaking my heart over this story [*OCS*], and cannot bear to finish it'.

25 CD and JF call on Macready, and they all walk in Hyde Park.

31 Gives a New Year's Eve dinner for various friends.

1841

January

6 (Wed) CD finishes the thirty-eighth number (chs 69–70) of *OCS*. At about this time he writes to Macready: 'I am slowly murdering that poor child [Nell], and grow wretched over it'. A

day or two later, having begun the thirty-ninth number (chs 71–2), he tells JF, 'Nobody will miss her like I shall.'

?17 Finishes *OCS* at 4 a.m.

21 Macready calls on CD and they both visit Rogers. Macready asks CD 'to spare the life of Nell in his story' (Macready's diary).

22 CD meets Captain Marryat at a dinner at Stanfield's.

26 Dines with JF.

27 Dines with Stanfield.

28 '. . . sat and *thought* all day; not writing a line; . . . imaged forth a good deal of *Barnaby* by keeping my mind steadily upon him' (to JF, 29 Jan). At about this time he tells Mitton of 'the extreme difficulty of fixing my thoughts on Barnaby after so recently shutting up the "Shop'".

29 Dines with Harness and afterwards attends an evening party at Miss Coutts's.

31 Dines with Rogers.

February

2 (Tues) Dines at Miss Coutts's.

3 Dines with Dr Southwood Smith.

4 Dines with Ainsworth.

6 Publication of the final number of *OCS*. CD dines with Cattermole at the Athenaeum.

8 Birth of Walter Landor Dickens, fourth child of CD.

13 First instalment of *BR* is published in *MHC*; 41 further weekly instalments to 27 November.

24 Goes to Brighton with Catherine (Old Ship Hotel).

25 Works at ch. 10 of *BR* and is 'blessed with a clear view of the end of the volume' (i.e. the second volume of *MHC*, which ends with ch. 12 of *BR*) (to JF).

March

3 (Wed) CD and Catherine return to London.

8 The main London newspapers carry a notice, inserted by CD's solicitors on his instructions, disclaiming responsibility for debts incurred by anyone bearing his surname – in other words, his father. CD works on a preface for a new edition of *OT*.

22 Dines with Macready.

April

3 (Sat) Goes with Macready to the Marquis of Northampton's;

among those present are Elliotson, Rogers, Stanfield and Henry Crabb Robinson.

10 Gives a dinner to those involved in the production of *MHC* to celebrate the appearance of the second volume of the work, published on or about 12 April.

26 Visits Tothill Fields Prison with Francis Smedley, to see William Jones, an errand-boy convicted of entering Buckingham Palace. Gives a dinner at which the guests include Fonblanque, Bulwer Lytton, Jeffrey and Rogers.

29 Tells JF that progress with *BR* is very slow.

May

4 (Tues) Jeffrey writes to Lord Cockburn that he and CD 'have struck up what I mean to be an eternal and intimate friendship. He lives very near us here, and I often run over and sit an hour *tête à tête*, or take a long walk in the park with him. . . .' CD also meets Hood during this year.

8 Dines with Ainsworth; JF is also present.

12 Sees 'the Magnetic boy', Alexis Didier, a young Belgian medium, at Townshend's house and later describes him as *'marvellous'* (to the Countess of Blessington, 2 June). Speaks at the Literary Fund dinner.

June

19 (Sat) CD and Catherine leave London to visit Scotland. They spend the 20th with the Smithsons at Easthorpe Hall, near Malton, Yorkshire; then continue northwards, reaching Edinburgh on the 22nd and remaining there (Royal Hotel) until 4 July.

23 CD visits 'the Parliament-house' and is 'introduced (I hope) to everybody in Edinburgh' (to JF). In the evening he and Catherine go to the Adelphi Theatre.

24 Attends a dinner and evening party at Lord Murray's.

25 A dinner is held in CD's honour at the Waterloo Rooms. Professor John Wilson ('Christopher North') is in the chair. 'It was the most brilliant affair you can conceive; the completest success possible, from first to last' (to JF, 26 June). According to CD (to Cattermole, 26 June), there are 250–70 guests present, as well as nearly 200 ladies who (in accordance with current custom) do not dine but enter the gallery in order to hear the speeches.

26 Dines with Lord Rutherfurd, the Lord Advocate; spends the night at Lord Jeffrey's, and dines there on the 27th.

28 Dines at Dr William Alison's (Alison is medical professor at Edinburgh University and campaigner for the relief of poverty).

29 CD is 'voted . . . by acclamation the freedom of the city' (to JF, 30 June). He dines at the home of William Allan, historical painter, who had made a sketch of him at the dinner on the 25th.

30 Breakfasts with Macvey Napier, editor of the *Edinburgh Review*; dines with Alexander and Robert Blackwood, publishers; attends an evening party given by William Drysdale, Treasurer of the Edinburgh Town Council; attends 'supper with all the artists' (to JF, 30 June).

July

1 (Thurs) Attends a lunch given by Thomas Maitland, Solicitor-General; dines with Lord Gillies, judge; attends evening party given by Joseph Gordon, Writer to the Signet.

2 Attends a dinner and evening party given by Patrick Robertson, advocate and wit.

3 Dines at Lord Jeffrey's; goes afterwards to the Adelphi theatre, where the orchestra plays 'Charley is my Darling' on his entrance; his appearance has been promised by newspaper reports, and the house is packed.

4 CD and Catherine, accompanied by their London servant Tom and by Angus Fletcher, advocate, leave Edinburgh for a tour of the Highlands, following a route made out for them by Lord Murray. They proceed first to Callander, via Stirling, and spend the night at Stewart's Hotel, nine miles from Callander. In the evening, CD walks to Loch Katrine.

5 They continue to Lochearnhead and remain there for three nights 'to rest and work' (to JF, 30 June), CD continuing with *BR*.

8 They leave Lochearnhead in the evening and spend the night at Killin.

9 They proceed to Ballachulish, 'a journey of between 50 and 60 miles, through the bleakest and most desolate part of Scotland' (to JF, 9 July), via Glencoe ('perfectly *terrible*').

10 CD abandons his intention of going to Oban on account of bad weather, and returns via Glencoe to Tyndrum; thence they go via Dalmally to Inverary. This time Glencoe is 'perfectly

horrific' (to JF, 11 July – a letter in which CD is eloquent on the wildness and dangers of the scene).

12 CD declines an invitation to attend a dinner in his honour at Glasgow.

13 Visits Glasgow and spends the night at Hamilton.

14–15 Spends two nights at Melrose and visits Dryburgh.

17 Spends the night at York. The first number of *Punch* is advertised in *MHC*.

18 Arrives back in London.

21 Cattermole, JF, Maclise and Macready dine with CD.

23 Is 'horribly hard at work' on *BR* (to Townshend) – probably on chs 49–50.

28 Dines with Townshend; Dr Elliotson is also present and mesmerises a patient.

30 Visits Belvedere and afterwards dines at Greenwich with JF, Cattermole, Macready, Maclise and others.

31 The Dickens children go to Broadstairs.

August

1 (Sun) CD and Catherine join the children in Broadstairs; they remain there until 2 October, but CD makes frequent visits to London during this period.

5 'I am warming up very much about *Barnaby*' (to JF): he is evidently at work on chs 55–6.

7 Publishes a poem, 'The Fine Old English Gentleman', in *The Examiner* (and others on the 14th and 21st).

11 'I have another number [of *BR*] ready, all but two slips' (to JF): that is, chs 57–8 are nearly finished. CD tells Mitton that, apart from two days, he has been 'constantly at work' since reaching Broadstairs.

21 Visits London, calls on Mitton, and has a meeting with Chapman and Hall in JF's chambers in Lincoln's Inn.

September

11 (Sat) Chs 63–4 of *BR* are finished.

19 Tells JF that he has made up his mind to go to America as soon after Christmas as possible; within a week, 4 January is named to JF as a possible date for departure.

21 Asks Macready's advice whether they should take the children to America. (Macready is against it, and his advice is followed.)

?22 Tells JF that he has informed Chapman and Hall that he will 'keep a note-book' during his visit to America and publish it on his return. Plans for the American visit go ahead rapidly, and on the 26th CD tells his brother Frederick that all arrangements for the voyage have been made.

October

2 (Sat) to 5 CD visits Rochester, Cobham and Gravesend with JF.

5 Back in London; falls ill, and on the 8th submits to 'a cruel operation' for fistula (to Beard, 12 Oct).

11 Macready and Browning visit CD and find him 'going on very comfortably' (Macready's diary).

12 CD tells a correspondent that he is weak but making a rapid recovery.

17 Still 'on the Sofa' (to Mitton) and dictating rather than writing his letters.

18 Death of Catherine Thomson, grandmother of Catherine Dickens.

24 Sudden death of George Thomson Hogarth, CD's brother-in-law, aged twenty. CD tells Mrs Hogarth (mother of the deceased) that he will place Mary Hogarth's grave at her disposal if she wishes to have her son buried there; the next day he tells JF, 'It is a great trial to me to give up Mary's grave. . . . I cannot bear the thought of being excluded from her dust.'

November

5 (Fri) Finishes *BR*.

6–20 In Windsor (White Hart Hotel) for rest and convalescence.

16 'I thank God I am getting stout and hearty, and can walk about the Parks here' (to Angus Fletcher).

24 Reports himself to Miss Coutts as 'quite well'.

December

4 (Sat) The last weekly number of *MHC* appears. CD gives a party at which the guests include Elliotson, Landor, Maclise, Macready, Stanfield and Talfourd, after the christening of Walter Landor Dickens at St Marylebone parish church.

11 Dines at Talfourd's.

14 Tells Murdo Young that he is living 'in a perpetual state of Weighing Anchor'. Throughout this month, and in view of his impending departure for America, CD's social life is hectic,

and on the 27th he tells Samuel Joseph that 'every hour of my time, this week, is fully occupied.'

15   The third volume of *MHC* is published. One volume editions of *OCS* and *BR* appear on the same day.
18   The Talfourds dine at CD's home.
23   Dines at Chapman's.
24   With JF, attends a rehearsal of Macready's *The Merchant of Venice* at Drury Lane.

1842

January
2   (Sun) CD and Catherine travel to Liverpool (Adelphi Hotel).
4   The *SS Britannia* sets sail for Boston under Captain Hewitt; CD and his wife are accompanied by Anne Brown, Catherine's maid. It is 'a most miserable voyage' (to Frederick Dickens, 30 Jan), CD being seasick for five days and Catherine for six.
20   They land at Halifax, where CD receives an enthusiastic welcome, then embark again for Boston.
22   Arrival in Boston, where they stay at the leading hotel, Tremont House, until 5 February.
23   CD receives the 'Young Men of Boston', a group formed to invite him to a public dinner (see 1 Feb).
24   Visits the State Capitol and attends a performance at the Tremont Theatre.
25   Begins sittings for Francis Alexander, portrait-painter (portrait now in Boston Museum of Fine Arts).
26   Begins sittings for Henry Dexter, sculptor (cast of the bust is in Dickens House); attends ball at Papanti's Hall.
29   Speaks at a presentation to Captain Hewitt; visits the Perkins Institute for the Blind and other institutions (see *AN*, ch. 3); writes to JF that 'We are already weary, at times, past all expression'.
30   Hears a sermon at the Seamen's Bethel (see *AN*, ch. 3); takes a long walk to see the sights of Boston with Charles Sumner and H. W. Longfellow.
31   Meets R. H. Dana; goes to National Theatre.

February
1   (Tues) Banquet given in CD's honour at Papanti's Hall.

5 Leaves Boston for Worcester, Massachusetts, where he stays with the Governor of Massachusetts, John Davis.

7 To Springfield, Massachusetts, by train, then proceeds to Hartford, Connecticut, by steamboat; during the stay in Hartford he visits the Insane Asylum, the Institution for the Deaf and Dumb, the State Prison, and the jail for untried offenders (see *AN*, ch. 5). CD's thirtieth birthday.

8 Guest of honour at a public dinner held at City Hotel, Hartford.

11 Arrives in New Haven, Connecticut, at 8 p.m., receives Yale students and professors at his hotel (the Tontine), and shakes hands with 'considerably more than five hundred people'.

12 To New York by steamboat; meets Cornelius Felton on board; arrives in New York at 2.30 p.m.; stays at Carlton House Hotel, Broadway (remains in New York until 5 Mar).

14 'Boz Ball' given in CD's honour.

15 'In bed all day with a violent sore throat' (to L. G. Clark).

16 Still unwell and cancels appearance at 'repeat performance' of ball.

18 Guest of honour at a dinner held at City Hotel, with Washington Irving in the chair. Announces that he will accept no more invitations to 'public entertainments'.

22 Meets William Cullen Bryant. 'I am sick to death of the life I have been leading here – worn out in mind and body – and quite weary and distressed' (to Jonathan Chapman).

24 Continues a letter to JF begun on the 17th, expressing his views on the copyright question.

27 Visits asylum, workhouse and City Penitentiary (see *AN*, ch. 6).

March

1 (Tues) Since Catherine is suffering from a sore throat, CD postpones their departure for Philadelphia.

2 Visits the Tombs (New York House of Detention) (see *AN*, ch. 6).

5 Leaves New York by train at 5 p.m. and arrives in Philadelphia at 11 p.m. During his three days in that city, spends one day visiting the Eastern Penitentiary.

9 Leaves Philadelphia at 6 a.m. by steamboat; later transfers to train; crosses the Susquehanna by boat; then proceeds by train to Baltimore and Washington, arriving in the latter city at 6.30 p.m. (Fuller's Hotel).

10 Calls on President Tyler and visits the Senate and House of

Representatives (see *AN*, ch. 8). On 15 March he tells JF that he goes to the House of Representatives every day.

14 Speaks at a private dinner given in his honour.

15 Attends a reception given by the President, having declined an invitation to dinner.

16 Leaves Washington after dining with Irving, who weeps *'heartily'* when they part (to JF, 17 Mar).

17 Arrives in Richmond, Virginia (the journey is described in *AN*, ch. 9), and finds the sight of slavery 'odious' (to Fonblanque, ?21 Mar). During his stay in Richmond, meets the actor Edwin Forrest.

18 Speaks at a 'social supper' given in his honour.

20 Arrives back in Washington.

21 At 4 p.m. leaves Washington for Baltimore (Barnum's Hotel).

22 On this day of rest he writes letters to friends in England totalling at least 8000 words.

24 Leaves Baltimore at 8.30 a.m. by train and travels to York, Pennsylvania, then by stagecoach to Harrisburg, Pennsylvania (Eagle Hotel).

25 Visits the State Capitol; leaves Harrisburg at 3 p.m. by canal boat for Pittsburgh.

28 Arrives in Pittsburgh in the evening and finds it 'like Birmingham' (to JF, 1 Apr). During his time in the city, visits the Western Penitentiary.

April

4 (Mon) Arrives in Cincinnati early in the morning and finds it 'a very beautiful city' (to JF, 15 Apr).

5 At a party given by Judge Timothy Walker, CD is introduced to 'at least one hundred and fifty first-rate bores' (to JF, 15 Apr).

6 Leaves Cincinnati and travels by steamboat down the Mississippi ('the beastliest river in the world': to JF, 15 Apr; *cf. AN*, ch. 12), arriving in Louisville shortly after midnight.

7 Departs at 1 p.m. by the steamer *Fulton* for St Louis, via Cairo (the 'Eden' of *MC*).

10 Arrives in St Louis.

11 Sight-seeing in St. Louis.

12 Visits Looking-Glass Prairie, St Clair County (see *AN*, ch. 13), and finds it less impressive than Salisbury Plain; spends the night at Mermaid Hotel, Lebanon.

13 Returns to St Louis about noon; attends a soirée and ball given in his honour ('very crowded': to JF, 15 Apr).

14 Leaves St Louis at 4 p.m.

17 Spends the night in Louisville.

18 Departs at 11 a.m. by the mail-boat *Benjamin Franklin*.

19 Arrives back in Cincinnati at 1 a.m.

20 Leaves Cincinnati at 8 a.m. by mail coach for Columbus.

21 Arrives in Colombus at 7 a.m.; holds a levee that evening.

22 Sets off at 7 a.m. by hired coach for Sandusky; much of this uncomfortable journey is by 'corduroy road' (see *AN*, ch. 14).

23 Arrives in Sandusky at 6 p.m. (Steamboat Hotel).

24 Spends the night in Cleveland.

25 'The people poured on board, in crowds, by six on Monday morning, to see me' (to JF, 26 Apr).

26 Travels from Buffalo to Niagara Falls by rail; is greatly impressed by the Falls and stays there for eight days.

May

1 (Sun) 'We have had a blessed Interval of quiet in this beautiful place [Niagara]' (to Henry Austin).

4 Leaves Niagara Falls, crosses Lake Ontario by steamboat, and arrives in Toronto.

6 Leaves Toronto by boat at noon.

7 Arrives in Kingston at 8 a.m.

10 Leaves Kingston at 9.30 a.m. and travels by a combination of St Lawrence steamboat and stagecoach.

11 Arrives in Montreal (Rasco's Hotel).

25 Appears in three plays with the Garrison Amateurs at the Queen's Theatre, Montreal (private performance).

28 Public performance with the Garrison Amateurs at the Theatre Royal.

30 Leaves Montreal and travels via St John's, Lake Champlain, Whitehall and Albany to New York.

June

2 (Thurs) Arrives in New York at 5 a.m. Makes an excursion up the North River to Hudson (see *AN*, ch. 15).

3 Spends the night at Lebanon Springs.

4 Visits a Shaker Village but finds the chapel closed.

7 CD and Catherine sail in the *George Washington* under Captain Ambrose Burrows, Jr.

29   They land at Liverpool and proceed straight to London for the reunion with their children: 'I never in my life felt so keenly as on the night of our reaching [home]' (to Jonathan Chapman, 3 Aug). Charley falls into violent convulsions and doctors are summoned, but he soon recovers.

30   The Dickens family move back into 1 Devonshire Terrace.

July

1   (Fri) Talfourd's Copyright Act receives royal assent.

9   CD's friends give a dinner at Greenwich, organised by JF, to welcome him home; among those present are Barham, Cruikshank, JF, Hood, Maclise, Marryat, Milnes, Procter, Stanfield and Talfourd.

11   '. . . the correspondence I have to get through just now (to say nothing of my American Sketches that may be just shaping themselves in my head . . .' (to H. P. Smith).

12   Entertains JF, Landor, Maclise and Macready to dinner: 'Dickens had been mesmerising his wife and Miss Hogarth, who had been in violent hysterics' (Macready's diary).

16   Gives dinner for Ainsworth and Marryat.

23   Goes to the Royal Academy Summer Exhibition and admires Maclise's painting of Hamlet.

25   A long letter from CD concerning the Mines and Collieries Bill appears in the *Morning Chronicle*.

26   Maclise dines at CD's home. CD writes to Macvey Napier that he has 'resolved to describe my American journies, in a couple of volumes; and am consequently, just now, very closely engaged'.

29   Tells Mitton that he will be busy all day working on *American Notes*. He shows the first chapter to Macready on the 29th, and the first four chapters seem to have been finished by the end of this month.

August

1   (Mon) The Dickens family leave London to spend two months in Broadstairs, 'a very delicious place' (to Jonathan Chapman, 3 Aug). For CD it is, as usual, a working holiday, the composition of *AN* continuing.

7   'I have been reading Tennyson all the morning on the seashore' (to JF), presumably the 1842 *Poems*.

10   Begins ch. 6 of *AN*. Later in the month he asks JF's opinion of

the title *American Notes for General Circulation*. Ch. 7 is finished and ch. 8 begun before the end of the month.

September
1 (Thurs) Spends 'a day or two' in London, leaving his family at the seaside.
14 Ch. 14 of *AN* is finished by this date and ch. 16 by the end of the month.

October
1   (Sat) The Dickens family return to London.
4   Finishes ch. 17 of *AN* at midnight.
5   Longfellow arrives as a guest, having been expected on the 10th CD dines with JF and they go to see Macready in Byron's *Marino Faliero* at Drury Lane.
6   CD takes Longfellow to Drury Lane to see Macready in *As You Like It*. During Longfellow's stay he takes him on expeditions to Cobham and Rochester, 'to the prisons', 'among tramps and thieves in the Mint lodging-houses' (letter of 13 Oct), and to Gore House to be introduced to Lady Blessington and Count D'Orsay.
18 CD and Longfellow breakfast with Rogers.
19 Publication of *AN*.
20 Departure of Longfellow, CD and JF accompanying him to Bristol (via Bath, where they call on Landor) to see him off on the 21st.
24 CD goes to Drury Lane to see Macready in *King John*.
27 CD sets off for Cornwall with JF, Maclise and Stanfield. After visiting Landor in Bath, he arrives in Exeter by train on the evening of the 29th and stays at the New London Inn; he visits his father at Alphington, then sets off for Plymouth and Land's End, probably via Marazion (for St Michael's Mount), Liskeard, Bodmin and Truro. The route back to Exeter includes a detour to Tintagel: in a letter of 22 October to Dr Southwood Smith he has expressed a wish to see 'the very dreariest and most desolate portion' of the Cornish coast, and Smith has recommended Tintagel. Later CD writes of the Cornish visit, 'I do believe there never was such a trip' (to Felton, 31 Dec). His original intention is to set the opening of his new novel on some desolate rocky coast, but he soon abandons the idea.

November

3 (Thurs) In Exeter again on the way home.

4 Back in London again by about this date.

11 Goes with Cruikshank to the funeral of William Hone (died 8 Nov) at Abney Park Cemetery, Stoke Newington.

12 Tells Miss Coutts that he is 'in the agonies of plotting and contriving a new book [*MC*]'. On the same day he sends to JF the tentative title *The Life and Adventures of Martin Chuzzlewig* (*sic*). He makes an offer to Macready to write a prologue for J. W. Marston's *The Patrician's Daughter*, and drafts the prologue during the next two weeks; the production opens on 10 December.

15 Commissions W. P. Frith to paint two small pictures: one of Dolly Varden, the other of Kate Nickleby.

20 Hears the Rev. Edward Tagart preach at the Unitarian Chapel in Little Portland Street; CD subsequently takes sittings in the chapel for himself and his family, and often attends services there. D'Orsay, Fonblanque and Maclise dine with CD.

25 Has been 'thrown . . . into a perfect passion of sorrow' by reading Browning's play *A Blot in the 'Scutcheon* (to JF).

26 *MC* is advertised in the *Athenaeum*.

27 Dines at Fonblanque's home.

December

1 (Thurs) Tells Mitton that he has received 'an immense [number] of letters from America [concerning *AN*]', and that 'The effect of the book on the better orders is *decidedly favourable.*'

2 Dines at Gore House.

6 Dines at the home of Thomas Hood, Maclise also being present.

8 The first number of *MC* is 'nearly done' (to JF) but in the event is not finished until about the 17th of this month.

24 Attends a rehearsal of Macready's pantomime *Harlequin and William Tell* at Drury Lane (and probably writes the review of it published in *The Examiner* on the 31st).

28 Dines at Gore House.

29 Tells Longfellow that the sales of *AN* have been 'enormous' (for details, see Patten, *CD and his Publishers* pp. 131–2).

31 First number of *MC* appears; serialisation continues to 30 June 1844.

During this month CD's parents move to Blackheath; later they move again to Lewisham.

1843

January

6 (Fri) Party at CD's home to celebrate Twelfth Night and Charley's sixth birthday: CD entertains the company with a magic lantern and conjuring-tricks. (Such a party becomes for many years a tradition in the Dickens household.)

8 'Hammering away' at the second number of *MC* (to JF).

16 Publishes a letter in *The Times* on the international copyright question.

20 Dines at Jack Straw's Castle, Hampstead, with Henry Austin and Mitton.

21–4 CD and Catherine visit Bath.

29 Thackeray comes to dinner.

31 Second number of *MC* appears.

February

6 (Mon) CD repeats his Twelfth Night conjuring-performance for the sons of Mrs Norton.

15 Catherine has for some time been 'exceedingly unwell' (to Ebenezer Johnston).

18 Finishes the third number of *MC*.

20 'The thought of him [CD's father] besets me, night and day; and I really do not know what is to be done with him' (to Mitton).

21 Goes to Dulwich College Picture Gallery with Mitton, and in the evening to a ball at the Procters'.

24 Goes to Drury Lane Theatre with Captain Hewitt to see Macready's benefit performance of *Much Ado about Nothing* and *Comus*. (CD reviews *Much Ado* in The *Examiner* on 4 Mar).

?27 Goes to the theatre with Stanfield, probably to Drury Lane to see Macready's *Hamlet*.

March

2 (Thurs) 'I shall be glad to hear of any improvement in [the sales of] Chuzzlewit' (to Chapman and Hall; sales of the early numbers have been disappointing). Tells Felton that he is 'in great health and spirits, and powdering away at Chuzzlewit, with all manner of facetiousness rising up before me as I go on'.

6 Is 'perfectly stricken down' by reading the Second Report of the Children's Employment Commission (to Dr Southwood Smith).

Later in the month, seeking peace and quiet in which to work on *MC*, he rents Cobley's Farm, Bow Lane, North Finchley, then in the country (on site of what is now 70 Queen's Avenue); this remains his base for several weeks, though he visits London as business requires.

April

2 (Sun) The Dickens's wedding anniversary and JF's birthday: they all dine together at the Star and Garter, Richmond.

4 CD presides at a dinner of the Printers' Pension Society.

12 Blanchard, JF, Jerrold, Lemon, Macready, Serle and Stanfield dine with CD.

24 CD solicits Miss Coutts's help in finding employment for his brother Alfred.

27 FitzGerald, Tennyson and Thackeray dine with CD.

May

1 (Mon) The sixth number of *MC* is finished by this date. CD attends a charity dinner in aid of Charterhouse Square Infirmary and is repelled by the speeches and sentiments of 'your City aristocracy. . . . Sleek, slobbering, bow-paunched, overfed, apoplectic, snorting cattle' (to Jerrold, 3 May).

3 Tells Jerrold that he is 'writing a little history of England for my boy [Charley]': this work (designed to prevent the boy's acquiring 'any conservative or High church notions') has not survived, but CD publishes a *Child's History of England* in 1851–3.

5 Dines with JF; they go afterwards to Drury Lane Theatre to see Macready in *Comus*.

6 Speaks at a dinner in aid of the Hospital for Consumption and Diseases of the Chest.

7 Sixth anniversary of Mary Hogarth's death: 'she is so much in my thoughts at all times (especially when I am successful, and have prospered in anything)' (to Mrs Hogarth, 8 May).

8 Dines at Greenwich with Ainsworth, JF, Jerdan, Landseer, Maclise, Macready and others.

23 Speaks at a dinner for the Charitable and Provident Society for the Aged and Infirm Deaf and Dumb.

28 Dines with Macready; the other guests include JF, Maclise and Stanfield.

June

7 (Wed) CD is working on chs 16–17 of *MC*.

14 Goes to see Macready in *Macbeth*, the final performance at Drury Lane Theatre under Macready's management.

19 Attends the presentation of a 'Testimonial' (a piece of plate) to Macready by the Duke of Cambridge, to honour his services to the English stage.

29 Speaks at a dinner in aid of 'The Sanatorium', founded by Dr Southwood Smith.

July

?1 (Sat) Goes to Yorkshire on holiday, staying with Mr and Mrs Charles Smithson at Easthorpe Park, near Malton, 'the most remarkable place of its size in England and immeasurably the most beautiful' (to Maclise, 6 July).

?6 Writes to ask JF's opinion of Mrs Gamp: 'I mean to make a mark with her'. (Ch. 19 of *MC*, in which Mrs Gamp makes her appearance, is evidently in proof by this stage.)

8 Visits Scarborough.

?17 Returns to London.

25 Sits for Miss Margaret Gillies, miniaturist. Agrees to act as chairman of a committee to raise money for the seven orphaned children of Edward Elton, an actor who has been drowned at sea; the next day, in a burst of epistolary activity, he solicits the help of Miss Coutts and others (eleven letters on this subject written on the 26th survive). (See also 3–4 Aug).

28 At work on the September number (chs 21–3) of *MC*: is getting on 'but slowly' (to JF).

August

?1 (Tues) Goes to Broadstairs for a two-month family holiday; work on *MC* continues

3–4 Briefly back in London to preside at a meeting of the committee raising money for the Elton children (see 25 July): well over £1000 has by now been raised.

13 'I have nearly killed myself with laughing at what I have done of the American No.' (to JF) – that is, chs 21–2 of *MC*.

14–15 In town again; calls on Thomas Mitton and dines with JF.

15 '. . . Martin has made them all stark staring raving mad across the water' (to JF): the reference is to the hostile reception by the American press of the seventh number (chs 16–17) of *MC*.

18 Completes the ninth number (chs 21–3) of *MC*; at about this time he sends instructions to Browne concerning the illustration for ch. 23.

25–6 In town again to visit the Elton children; on the 26th he calls on Miss Coutts and speaks at a farewell dinner for Macready, who is leaving for America, at the Star and Garter, Richmond.

During this month (date uncertain) CD picnics at 'a rural spot near Harrow' (letter of Lady Blessington) with Lady Blessington and Count D'Orsay; JF is also present.

September

 5 (Tues) A letter to Miss Coutts contains CD's first reference to the Ragged Schools: he tells her than on the 14th he will 'take my seat among the fluttering rags of Saffron Hill'.

14 Has finished ch. 25 of *MC* by this date. Goes to London and visits a Ragged School with Stanfield: 'and an awful sight it is. . . . I deem it an experiment most worthy of your charitable hand' (to Miss Coutts, 16 Sept). The visit is described in a letter to the *Daily News* (4 Feb 1846) and in 'A Sleep to Startle Us' (*HW*, 13 Mar 1852; repr. in *Miscellaneous Papers*).

17 Back in Broadstairs. 'The next Number [of *MC*: the sixth, containing chs 24–6] bangs all the others!' (to Mitton).

28 CD's father is again in debt and has sent him 'a threatening letter': 'I am amazed and confounded by the audacity of his ingratitude. He, and all of them, look upon me as something to be plucked and torn to pieces for their advantage. . . . My soul sickens at the thought of them' (to Mitton).

October

 3 (Tues) The Dickens family return to London from Broadstairs. Early in this month, CD begins works on *A Christmas Carol*.

 4 Goes to Manchester with Mitton and (5th) speaks at the first annual soirée of the Athenaeum in the Free Trade Hall. They stay (4th–6th) with Mr and Mrs Henry Burnett.

 6 Leaves Manchester and visits Liverpool.

 8 Returns to London.

24 Sits again for Miss Gillies (see 25 July).

November

10 (Fri) Tells JF that he has been 'all day in *Chuzzlewit* agonies –

conceiving only': he is working on the twelfth number (chs 30–2).

19 Tells JF that he 'blazed away till 9 last night; only stopping ten minutes for dinner! I suppose I wrote eight printed pages of *Chuzzlewit* yesterday' (i.e. the latter part of ch. 31); 'making myself laugh very much [over ch. 32]'.

20 Tells JF that he has 'grave thoughts of keeping my whole menagerie in Italy, three years'.

25 Is 'full of Grief' over his father's financial irresponsibility.

29 Tells Miss Marion Ely that he has been 'working from morning until night upon my little Christmas Book': *CC* is finished by the end of the month.

December

2 (Sat) CD gives a dinner for Fonblanque, Sydney Smith, Barham, JF, Maclise, Rogers and others.

9 Gives a dinner for Ainsworth, Cruikshank, JF, Maclise, Thackeray and others.

17 'I was writing this Morning until Three o'Clock' (to Maclise): the reference is to the thirteenth number (chs 33–5) of *MC*.

19 Publication of *CC*; CD sends presentation copies to Ainsworth, Carlyle, Miss Coutts, Fonblanque, JF, Landor, Rogers, Talfourd, Thackeray and others.

24 Hears from Chapman and Hall that *CC* is 'in its Sixth Thousand' (to Mitton, 27 Dec).

1844

January

2 (Tues) Tells Mitton that 9000 copies of *CC* have now been printed.

3 Tells Macready that *CC* has been 'a most prodigious success – the greatest, I think, I have ever achieved'.

6 A second edition of *CC* is advertised. A Twelfth Night party is held at the Dickens home; CD performs as a conjuror.

9 Begins an action against the printers and publishers responsible for pirating an abridged edition of *CC* in the series *Parley's Illuminated Library* (the action is dropped in May).

15 Birth of Francis Jeffrey Dickens, fifth child of CD.

20 Third edition of *CC* is advertised.

30 Visits Bath and dines with Landor.

February

10 (Sat) to 11 Has a troubled night after discovering that his earnings on the first 6000 copies of *CC* amount to only £230: 'And the last four [thousand] will yield as much more. I had set my heart and soul upon a Thousand [pounds], clear' (to JF, 11 Feb).

20 Goes to the Adelphi Theatre to see Edward Stirling's dramatic version of *CC*, having previously attended rehearsals. (The piece opened on 5 Feb and ran until 9 Mar). ·

25 Shortly after finishing the fourteenth number of *MC*, CD goes to Liverpool, where (26th) he speaks at a soirée of the Mechanics' Institution. He sees his sister Fanny; revisits the *Britannia* (on which he had sailed to America in 1842, and which is lying in the harbour); and dines with Captain Hewitt. He also sees Christiana Weller, whose performance on the piano he has introduced at the soirée; invites himself to lunch with her family; and sends her a 'bit of doggerel' concluding, 'I love her dear name which has won me some fame, / But Great Heaven how gladly I'd change it!'

28 Leaves Liverpool for Birmingham, where he speaks that evening at the conversazione of the Polytechnics Institution.

29 Returns to London.

March

2 (Sat) Dines with Maclise.

10 Enquires of Lady Blessington whether Nice is a healthy, cheap and pleasant place of residence: he means 'to decamp, bag and baggage, next midsummer, for a twelvemonth'.

11 Receives a letter from T. J. Thompson, announcing that he is in love with Christiana Weller (see 25 Feb); CD writes back saying that, in Thompson's place, he 'would win her if I could, by God'.

19 Is now thinking of Pisa as a place of residence (to Count D'Orsay). Five days later he tells Angus Fletcher that he intends to transport his household to Italy for twelve months.

29 Congratulates Thompson on winning Christiana's hand ('a noble prize').

April

2 (Tues) The customary dinner is held at Richmond to celebrate the Dickenses' wedding-anniversary and JF's birthday.

5   CD goes to Yorkshire to attend the funeral of Charles Smithson.
    He stays at Malton Abbey.
9   Visits Staithes and Whitby.
11 Returns to London.
17 Tells Mitton that he is 'very much and pressingly in want of a
    hundred pounds until June'.
20 Speaks at a dinner for the Governesses' Benevolent Institution.
23 CD and JF meet, as usual, to celebrate Shakespeare's birthday.
During this month CD writes 'Threatening Letter to Thomas Hood,
from an Ancient Gentleman. By Favour of Charles Dickens' for
Hood's Magazine, where it appears the following month.

May
11 (Sat) Speaks at the annual dinner of the Artists' Benevolent
    Society.
28 Lets 1 Devonshire Terrace to Mrs Sophia Onslow for one year.
    On the previous day, the Dickens family move to 9 Osnaburgh
    Terrace, off Albany Street, a temporary dwelling before going
    abroad.
31 Tells R. M. Milnes that he is 'finishing Chuzzlewit'.

June
4   (Tues) Speaks at a dinner in aid of The Sanatorium.
13 Attends a Soirée Musicale at the Hanover Square Rooms to hear
    Christiana Weller perform.
17 Visits Landor in Bath.
19 CD's friends give him a farewell dinner at the Trafalgar Tavern,
    Greenwich; among over forty present are Ainsworth, Browne,
    Cruikshank, Fonblanque, JF, Jerrold, Maclise, Milnes and
    Stanfield.
?22–4 Goes on a sailing-trip with Fonblanque.
30 Dines at JF's: Beard and Frederick Dickens are also present. The
    final number of *MC* is published.

July
2   (Tues) The Dickens family set off for Italy, accompanied by
    Georgina Hogarth, Louis Roche (courier), and servants – a
    party of twelve all told. They cross from Dover (where they
    spend the night of the 2nd) to Boulogne and spend two days in
    Paris (Hotel Meurice), 'the most extraordinary place in the
    world' (to D'Orsay, 7 Aug). Then they proceed to Chalons; go

by steamboat down the Rhône to Lyons; by road again to Aix and Marseilles, probably arriving in the latter city on 14 July and leaving on the 15th by boat for Genoa.

16 They arrive in Genoa and proceed to Albaro, where they stay at the Villa di Bagnerello (now the Villa Barabino), described in *Pictures from Italy*.

August

?10 (Sat) 'My paper is arranged, and my pens are spread out, in the usual form' (to JF): CD is planning to begin work on another Christmas book.

September

6 (Fri) CD leaves from Marseilles to meet his brother Frederick, who has come out from London on a visit.

12 CD and Frederick arrive in Albaro.

13 Frederick narrowly escapes drowning while swimming.

?23 The Dickens family leave the Villa di Bagnerello and move into the Palazzo Peschiere, Genoa. CD has as vivid dream of Mary Hogarth, the first since February 1838.

October

?8 (Tues) CD decides on *The Chimes* as the title of his new Christmas book: 'It's a great thing to have my title, and see my way how to work the bells' (to JF, 8 Oct). By about the middle of the month, he has his 'steam very much up' and is writing hard (undated letters quoted in JF's *Life*).

18 Sends JF the manuscript of the 'First Quarter' of *Chimes*, probably written 9–16 October.

?21 Sends JF the 'Second Quarter' of *The Chimes*; the 'Third Quarter' follows on or about the 29th.

November

3 (Sun) Finishes *The Chimes*.

5 Gives a dinner-party at which M and Mme Emile de la Rue are among the guests (see 23 Dec).

6–21 Tours Italy, accompanied by Roche; they visit Parma, Modena, Bologna, Ferrara, Venice (12th–13th), Verona, Mantua, Milan (18th–21st); then CD proceeds to England via Lake Maggiore, Simplon Pass, Vevey, Fribourg (23rd), Basle, Strasbourg (25th), arriving in Paris on the 28th after a fifty-hour journey in a 'horrible' coach (to Macready), and staying there at the Hotel Bristol. This tour of Italy provides material later for *Pictures from Italy*, which draws on letters written at the time.

30　Arrives in London; on arrival he 'rushed into the arms of Mac[ready] and Forster' (to Catherine, 2 Dec).

December
　3　(Tues) CD reads *The Chimes* after dinner in JF's chambers to a group of friends that includes Blanchard, Carlyle, Jerrold, Maclise, Stanfield and Frederick Dickens.

　5　Second reading of *The Chimes*; the audience this time includes Barham, Fonblanque, Maclise, Macready and Stanfield.

?9–13　In Paris with Macready. On the 11th they see Dumas's *Christine* at the Odéon. During this visit, CD meets Victor Hugo, Alexandre Dumas, Théophile Gautier, Eugène Delacroix, Eugène Sue and others. CD and Macready then proceed to Marseilles by *malle post*, arriving on the 17th and embarking for Genoa on the 19th.

16　Publication of *The Chimes*.

18　An authorised dramatisation of *The Chimes* by Gilbert A'Beckett and Mark Lemon opens at the Adelphi Theatre; other versions open in London on the 26th and 28th.

20　CD arrives in Genoa and is reunited with his family.

23　Begins to mesmerise Madame de la Rue, and does so frequently during the next few weeks.

1845

January
19　(Sun) CD leaves Genoa with Catherine for a tour of Italy. They visit Spezia, Carrara, Pisa, Siena, Leghorn and Rome, where they stay at the Hotel Meloni from 30 January to 6 February; in Rome they witness the Carnival, and CD visits the Coliseum repeatedly and walks in the Campagna. Then they proceed to Naples, where they stay at the Vittoria Hotel (2–26 Feb) and Georgina Hogarth joins them. From Naples they make excursions to Sorrento, Paestum, Pompeii and Herculaneum, and (21 Feb) ascend Vesuvius under hair-raising conditions. Like the previous one, this tour is described in *Pictures from Italy*.

March

2   (Sun) Back in Rome, CD finds a letter from JF announcing that their friend Samuel Laman Blanchard has committed suicide. Soon afterwards, he reads in the English newspapers of the death on 22 February of another friend, Sydney Smith. They remain in Rome, where they are joined by the de la Rues, until the 25th. On the return journey they visit Florence.

April

9   (Wed) They arrive back in Genoa.

June

9   (Mon) The Dickens family leave Genoa and proceed via Milan, Como, the St Gothard Pass, Zurich, Frankfurt, and down the Rhine to Cologne, to Brussels, where they are joined (27th) by JF, Maclise and Jerrold.

30   They leave Brussels for Ghent, Bruges and Ostend.

July

3   (Thurs) They arrive in London and return to 1 Devonshire Terrace.

Early in July CD tells JF that he has an idea for a weekly periodical to be called *The Cricket*; the idea is soon abandoned, but towards the end of the month he tells JF that the cricket would provide 'a delicate and beautiful fancy for a Christmas book'. At about the same time CD has an outing to Greenwich with a party that includes Catherine, Georgina and Christiana Weller.

August

During this month rehearsals take place for the plays staged on 20 September, and CD is much occupied with arrangements for the production.

15   (Fri) to 20   The Dickens family are on holiday at Broadstairs (Albion Hotel). The children remain there after CD and Catherine return to London, and CD visits them with Maclise from 30 August to 1 September.

September

CD's preoccupation with the theatricals continues to occupy much of his time during this month; on the 18th he describes himself to Miss Macready as 'half dead with Managerial work'.

20 (Sat) Performance of Ben Jonson's *Every Man in his Humour* at the Royalty Theatre, Dean Street, followed by Mrs Gore's farce *A Good Night's Rest*. This is a private performance to several hundred invited guests; but 'It got into the Papers, notwithstanding all our precautions' (to Mme de la Rue, 27 Sep), and it is reviewed in *The Times* and elsewhere. The audience includes Lady Holland, Lady Blessington, Count D'Orsay, Browning, Mrs Carlyle, Macready, Talfourd, Tennyson and the Duke of Devonshire. In Jonson's comedy, CD plays Bobadil, and the other actors include JF as Kitely and Frederick Dickens, Jerrold, Leech, Lemon, Mayhew and Stone. In the farce, CD and Lemon appear. After the performance, there is a supper for the cast and their wives at which Cattermole, D'Orsay and Macready are also present.

October
5 (Sun) to 6   CD is at Brighton (Bedford Hotel) with JF.
Before the middle of the month he is considering taking on the editorship of the *Daily News*.
18–19   CD visits Derbyshire, to see Joseph Paxton (one of the backers of the *Daily News*) at Chatsworth House.
20 Tells Mitton that he is 'trying to engage the best people, right and left' – that is, for the staff of the *Daily News*. The staff eventually includes Sidney Laman Blanchard, Fonblanque, JF, George Hogarth, Jerrold, Lemon, Wills and John Dickens.
21 Christiana Weller marries T. J. Thompson; CD makes a speech at the wedding-breakfast.
28 Birth of Alfred D'Orsay Tennyson Dickens (of whose name Edward FitzGerald later comments that it evinces CD's 'Snobbishness and Cockneyism').

November
3 (Mon) CD tells Bradbury and Evans that he is prepared to accept the post of editor of the *Daily News* at a salary of £2000 a year (double that which they have offered).
5 Rehearsal for a repeat performance of *Every Man in his Humour*; other rehearsals follow on 10 and 12 November.
15 Private performance of *Every Man in his Humour* at the St James's Theatre at the request of the Prince Consort, in aid of The Sanatorium.

December
1   (Mon) Tells Miss Coutts that he has 'just finished' *The Cricket on the Hearth*; describes himself to Joseph Paxton as 'regularly in harness' at the *Daily News* office at 90 Fleet Street.
13–17 In Liverpool on business for the *Daily News*.
19   Rehearsals begin for a performance of Fletcher and Massinger's *The Elder Brother*, adapted by JF, and R. B. Peake's farce *Comfortable Lodgings*.
20   Publication of *The Cricket on the Hearth*. A dramatisation of the story by Albert Smith opens at the Lyceum Theatre; another version opens at the Adelphi on the 30th, and within a month of publication versions are being played at seventeen different theatres.
30   Tells Mrs Hannah Brown that the sale of the *Cricket* is 'quite enormous' (but Patten notes [*CD and his Publishers*, pp. 167–8] that JF's statement that *Cricket* sales doubled those of *The Chimes* is an exaggeration: CD's profits from the two books were 'almost identical').
31   The first number of the revised edition of *OT* appears; further instalments follow at monthly intervals to 30 September 1846.

1846

January
2   (Fri) Macready visits JF's chambers and finds CD there trying on his costume for the play; Macready is distressed to 'hear of intemperate language' between CD and JF (Macready's diary).
3   Benefit performance of *The Elder Brother* (see 19 Dec 1845), in which the main roles are taken by CD and JF, and of *Comfortable Lodgings*, in aid of Miss Kelly. The Prologue to *The Elder Brother* has been written by CD.
6   The Dickenses' annual Twelfth Night party, which also celebrates Charley's birthday. The numerous guests include Cruikshank, JF, Landor, Macready, Marryat, Stanfield and Talfourd.
17   A dummy issue of the *Daily News* is produced.
21   The first issue of the *Daily News* appears. It includes an 'Address to the Reader' by CD, who also contributes the first of a series of 'Travelling Letters – Written on the Road', which appear irregularly until 11 March and utilise material that also appears

in *Pictures from Italy* (though the total series constitutes less than half the book). The humorous second leader is probably also by CD.

24 CD's poem 'The British Lion' appears in the *Daily News*.

30 CD tells Bradbury and Evans that he is 'thoroughly disgusted' by their treatment of him (they have cast doubts on the competence of one of the sub-editors whom he has chosen), and that it is 'extremely probable' that he will quit the newspaper. He also tells JF that he is thinking of 'going abroad to write a new book in shilling numbers'.

February
5 (Thurs) CD dines with Macready; the other guests include JF and Thackeray.

7–9 Visits Rochester and district with Catherine, Georgina, JF, Maclise and Jerrold; they spend two nights at the Bull Inn, Rochester, and visit 'the old Castle, Watts's Charity, and Chatham fortifications on the Saturday, passing Sunday in Cobham church and Cobham park' (JF, *Life*).

9 Resigns the editorship of the *Daily News*, but continues for a time to make occasional contributions.

14 Publishes poem 'The Hymn of the Wiltshire Labourers' in the *Daily News*.

23 Publishes the first of five letters on capital punishment in the *Daily News* (the others appear on 28 Feb and 9, 13 and 16 Mar).

March
1 (Sun) CD asks Lady Blessington and Count D'Orsay to lend him the letters he sent them from Italy: he has evidently resumed work on *Pictures from Italy*.

2 'Vague thoughts of a new book are rife within me just now; and I go wandering about at night into the strangest places, . . . seeking rest, and finding none' (to Lady Blessington).

22 Visits Ragged Schools.

April
1 (Wed) CD, Catherine and Georgina dine at the Star and Garter, Richmond, with JF, Maclise, Macready and Stanfield.

During this month, CD tells JF that he cannot 'shut out the paper [the *Daily News*] sufficiently' in London 'to write well', and that he intends to 'write my book [*Dombey and Son*] in Lausanne and in

Genoa', adding that by living 'in Switzerland for the summer, and in Italy or France for the winter', he will save money on household expenses. On the 22nd he mentions two further reasons for leaving England: he can write 'a long book . . . better in retirement', and he wants to 'get up some Mountain knowledge . . . for purposes of fiction.' He is seeking a tenant for his house.

6   Speaks at a dinner of the General Theatrical Fund.
18 Bradbury and Evans announce 'A NEW ENGLISH STORY, by Mr Dickens' as forthcoming.
21 Christening of Alfred D'Orsay Tennyson Dickens.
29 Calls on Miss Coutts, who is interesting herself in Charley's education and is prepared to make a financial contribution towards it.
28 Dines with Lady Blessington; the other guests include JF, Jerdan, Landseer and Macready.

May
 2 (Sat) Goes to the Royal Academy Exhibition with Macready, and attends the Royal Academy dinner with Macready, Landseer and Rogers. Afterwards CD goes to the Lyceum Theatre to see General Tom Thumb in Albert Smith's *Hop o' my Thumb*, accompanied by Stanfield and Talfourd as well as the three friends already mentioned.
 7 Dines with Macready; the other guests include Count D'Orsay, Landseer and the Procters.
18 Bradbury and Evans announce that the first number of the new novel will appear in October. Publication of *Pictures from Italy*; by 1 July, some 5000 copies have been sold and a reprint is called for (the so-called 'second edition' appears on 19 Sep).
21 Dines with Talfourd; the other guests include JF, Maclise, Macready and Stanfield.
26 In a long letter from CD to Miss Coutts there occurs the first reference to the project that later takes shape as Urania Cottage (see 5 June 1847).
29 CD and Catherine dine with JF – a farewell dinner.
30 They set off for Switzerland, accompanied by their children and by Georgina, Louis Roche, Catherine's maid Anne Brown, a cook and two nurse-maids. They travel via Ostend, Verviers, Coblenz, Mannheim and Strasbourg (where they spend the night of 7 June), and continue via Basle (8 June) to Lausanne, arriving there on 11 June and staying at the Hotel Gibbon.

June
15 (Mon) They move into a rented house, Rosemont (now demolished), 'a kind of beautiful bandbox' (to Maclise, 14 June), situated 'on the hill between Lausanne and Ouchy – about midway between the two places' (to D'Orsay, 5 Aug). (Tennyson has declined an invitation to share the house.)
29 Dines with Haldimand and meets the Hon. Richard Watson and his wife (Mrs Watson notes in her diary that she likes CD 'altogether very much' and finds him 'unaffected').
Before the end of the month, CD has written 'a good deal . . . for Lord John [Russell] about the Ragged schools', and 'a good deal for Miss Coutts, in reference to her charitable projects' (to JF, ?28 June), as well as writing half of *The Life of Our Lord*, a version of the Gospels for his children not intended for publication (published 1934). On or about the 27th he begins *D&S*, making 'a plunge straight over head and ears into the story' (ibid.). He is also beginning to think about his fourth Christmas book.

July
5 (Sun) CD tells JF that he is 'writing slowly' but has started the second chapter of *D&S* and hopes to finish the opening number (chs 1–4) within two weeks. He promises 'a great surprise' (i.e. the death of little Paul) at the end of the fourth number (in the event it is not until the end of the fifth that Paul dies). On the 18th, however, the first number is still not completed, and a projected trip to Chamonix has been postponed for a week.
6 Dines with Cerjat; Haldimand and the Watsons are also present.
16 The Watsons dine with CD, who is 'in extraordinary spirits and . . . very amusing' (Mrs Watson's diary).
18 Asks JF's opinion of *The Battle of Life* as a title for the new Christmas book.
25 Sends the manuscript of the first chapters of *D&S* to JF and gives him 'an outline of my immediate intentions in reference to *Dombey*', this important letter summarising the main action of the novel.
27 A party that includes CD and Catherine, Georgina, the Watsons, the Cerjats and Haldimand make 'an excursion by the Lac de Brêt to Vevey' (Mrs Watson's diary).
28 Accompanied by Catherine and Georgina, CD sets off for Chamonix; the night is spent at Martigny, and on the next day

they cross the Col de Balme, 'on mules *for ten hours at a stretch*' (to JF, 2 Aug).

30–31 At Chamonix.

August

1 (Sat) They return by the Tête Noire Pass, reaching Lausanne the next day. Early in the month, CD visits Chillon.

4 CD dines with the Watsons; Cerjat and Haldimand are also present.

10 CD and the ladies go on another outing organised by Watson to the Lac de Brêt and Vevey; among those also present are Cerjat and Haldimand.

11 The Watsons spend the evening with 'the Boz family' (Mrs Watson's diary); CD and Mrs Watson play at battledore and shuttlecock.

16 The Thompsons, who have arrived in Lausanne on the 10th, dine with CD and Catherine.

19 Accompanied by Haldimand and the Watsons, CD visits a home for the blind.

21 Dines with the Watsons; Haldimand and Cerjat are also present.

23 Tennyson and Edward Moxon, who are touring Switzerland, call on CD, who 'was very hospitable and gave us biscuits . . . and a flask of Liebfraumilch' (Tennyson to FitzGerald, 12 Nov).

25 Attends a regatta at Ouchy.

30 Tells JF that he is writing only slowly at *D&S* and feels desperately 'the absence of streets and numbers of figures' as a stimulus to his imagination. He also says that he will begin his Christmas book 'straightway' (but see 9 Sep), and that he has been 'dimly conceiving a very ghostly and wild idea, which I suppose I must now reserve for the *next* Christmas book' (this is the germ of *The Haunted Man*).

September

1 (Tues) CD, Catherine, Georgina, the Watsons, the Cerjats and Haldimand, with other friends and two servants, set off for the St Bernard convent. They spend the night at Martigny.

2 They continue via Orsières and Lyddes, and spend the night at the convent.

3 Back in Martigny.

4   Back in Lausanne. The trip later provides material for *Little Dorrit* (II, 1).

?7   Finishes the second number of *D&S*.

9   Begins *The Battle of Life*.

12   Reads the first number of *D&S* to a gathering of friends that includes the Watsons, the Cerjats, Haldimand, and the Thompsons (see also 10 Oct). Soon afterwards CD tells JF 'a great deal of money might possibly be made (if it were not infra dig) by one's having Readings of one's own books'.

?25   Tells JF that he fears 'there may be NO CHRISTMAS BOOK!': he has written 'nearly a third' of *The Battle of Life*, but is 'fearful of wearing myself out if I go on, and not being able to come back to [*D&S*] with the necessary freshness and spirit'.

26   Sets off for Geneva with Catherine, Georgina joining them there on about 1 October. Begins the second part of *The Battle of Life* on about 30 September, but is still inclined to abandon the idea of completing it in time for Christmas publication.

30   First number of *D&S* is published; monthly instalments continue to 31 March 1848.

October

3   (Sat) they return from Geneva to Lausanne. The Talfourds arrive at Rosemont for a two-day visit.

6   A revolt breaks out in Geneva; after two days, the government capitulates and a Radical president takes office.

10   CD sends to JF the first two parts of *The Battle of Life*. Bradbury and Evans print another 5000 copies of the first number of *D&S*, bringing the total so far to 30,000. CD reads the second number of the novel to a gathering of friends.

12   Tells Emile de la Rue that the opening number of *D&S* has been 'an immense success', and that he is about to embark on the third and final part of his Christmas book.

18   Sends the final part of *The Battle of Life*, finished the previous day, to JF.

19–28   In Geneva again with Catherine and Georgina.

31   'I am at work at [the third number of] Dombey with good speed, thank God' (to JF).

November

9   (Mon) Finishes the third number (chs 8–10) of *D&S*, chs 9–10 having been written in five days.

12   Reads *The Battle of Life* to the Watsons after dinner.
13   Returns the corrected proofs of *The Battle of Life* to JF.
14   The Dickenses dine with T. J. and Christiana Thompson.
15   The Dickenses dine with Haldimand, the Watsons also being present.
16   The Dickens family and servants leave Lausanne for Paris, travelling post in two carriages with a third for the luggage. Their route takes them via Auxonne, Montbard and Sens.
20   They arrive in Paris, staying temporarily at the Hotel Brighton but after a few days moving into a rented house at 48 rue de Courcelles.
?22   CD receives a letter from his father stating that his sister Fanny is suffering from consumption.

December
 6   (Sun) After some difficulties in settling to work again, CD has by this date written the first half of ch. 11 of *D&S* (i.e. the opening of the fourth number).
15   CD arrives in London, where he is involved with Albert Smith's authorised dramatisation of *The Battle of Life*, produced on the 21st, and followed by six other versions within the next few weeks. He is probably also busy with the proofs of the fourth number of *D&S*.
19   Publication of *The Battle of Life*: CD writes to Catherine, '23,000 copies already gone!!!' He attends a rehearsal of the stage version of the book until 2 a.m.
21   Dines at Macready's; the other guests include Elliotson, JF, Leech and Lemon.
23   Leaves London to return to Paris via Boulogne.
31   The Watsons dine with CD.

1847

January
?4   (Mon) CD tells JF that he is 'working very slowly' at *D&S*.
15   Finishes the fifth number of *D&S*, published at the end of the month. 'Between ourselves – Paul is dead. He died on Friday night [15th] at about 10 o'clock; and as I had no hope of getting to sleep afterwards, I went out, and walked about Paris until breakfast-time next morning' (to Miss Coutts, 18 Jan).

16 JF arrives in Paris, staying until the 31st, and goes sight-seeing
    'with a dreadful insatiability' (CD to Lady Blessington, 27 Jan).
    The two friends visit the Louvre, the Bibliothèque Royale,
    Versailles, St Cloud, the Opéra, the Morgue, and other places,
    including prisons and theatres.
17 CD and JF visit Victor Hugo.
25 The Watsons dine with CD; JF is also present.

February
4 (Thurs) CD resumes work on *D&S* and finds it 'very difficult
   indeed to fall into the new vein of the story' (to JF, 17 Feb, where
   he also explains that 'to transfer to Florence, instantly, all the
   previous interest, is what I am aiming at').
7 Dines at the British Embassy.
10 Sends ch. 18 of *D&S* to JF: 'I have taken the most prodigious
    pains with it'. (Ch. 18 was written before ch. 17.) He tells JF that
    'Paul's death has amazed Paris'.
12 Tells Frederick Dickens that he is 'desperately busy'.
19 Learning that the sixth number of *D&S* is two pages short, CD
    travels to London via Boulogne and Folkestone in order to deal
    with the situation, and is met in London by JF.
21 Dines with Lady Blessington at Gore House; Louis Napoleon
    and Charley Dickens are among the guests.
23 Leaves London.
24 Arrives back in Paris after spending the night at Boulogne.
?25 News reaches Paris, in a letter from JF, that Charley has fallen
    ill with scarlet fever on the 23rd and has been removed from
    King's College School, Wimbledon, by JF and Dr Elliotson and
    installed at his maternal grandmother's lodgings in Albany
    Street.
28 CD and Catherine, accompanied by Louis Roche, travel to
    London, where they spend several nights at the Victoria Hotel,
    Euston Square.

March
7 (Sun) Death of William Hall, of the firm of Chapman and Hall;
   CD later attends his funeral in Highgate Cemetery.
8 By this date, finding that the tenant of 1 Devonshire Terrace
   (whose lease runs until 31 May) is unwilling to vacate the
   house, CD and Catherine have moved into a rented house, 1
   Chester Place, Regent's Park. Charley is making a good

recovery but neither of his parents is allowed to visit him for fear of infection.

9　Work has not yet been started on this month's number of *D&S*: 'My wretchedness, just now, is inconceivable' (to Georgina Hogarth).

10　CD begins the seventh number of *D&S*. Macready calls and, having just read the fifth number, 'could not speak to [CD] for sobs' (Macready's diary).

18　CD is 'in the grip of Dombey' (to Ainsworth).

27　First weekly number of the Cheap Edition is published. CD goes to meet his children and Georgina, who have crossed from Paris under the escort of Louis Roche.

29　Speaks at the annual dinner of the General Theatrical Fund.

April

3　(Sat) Charley is withdrawn from King's College School for reasons of health.

?5　CD goes with Maclise to inspect a house in Hammersmith for possible use as 'Miss Coutts's Asylum' (see 5 June).

7　Goes to the Adelphi Theatre with Maclise and Stanfield to see J. B. Buckstone's melodrama *The Flowers of the Forest*: 'I question whether I have ever seen anything better' (to JF, 9 Apr).

10　JF and Tracey dine with CD.

18　Birth of Sydney Smith Haldimand Dickens, seventh child of CD: 'my dear Kate suffered terribly' (to Macready, 19 Apr).

19　Tells Macready that he has '*one half of the current Number yet to write*' (ch. 23 is finished, but chs 24–5 as yet unwritten).

24　Attends a reception given by Sir Robert Peel at his house in Whitehall Gardens

May

5　(Wed) CD and Macready call on Jenny Lind.

9　Dines with JF; Maclise, Macready and Stanfield are also among those present.

10　Tells Thomas Chapman that he has been 'very unwell these last few days, with a low dull nervousness of a most distressing kind' – presumably the after-effects of an accident on 3 May, when a horse 'made a sudden attack upon me in the stable' (to Lord Robertson, 6 May). Tells Miss Coutts that he has 'not the heart' to work at the current number of *D&S*.

13   Attends an amateur performance of Victor Hugo's *Hernani* at the St James's Theatre.

15   Dines with Macready; Landor, who is also present, notes that CD looks 'thin and poorly'.

17   CD and Catherine go to Brighton (until the 29th) and stay in lodgings at 148 King's Road. The ninth number of *D&S* is written there and finished on 23 May.

27   Goes to London, perhaps to deliver the manuscript or correct the proofs of the ninth number of *D&S*, and takes Mary and Kate Dickens back to Brighton with him.

29   Returns to London from Brighton with his wife and daughters.

30   Dines at Macready's home, where the other guests include JF, Jerrold, Jenny Lind, Bulwer Lytton, Maclise, the Procters and Wilkie.

June

3   (Thurs) Goes to Her Majesty's Theatre with Catherine, Georgina and Dr Elliotson to hear Jenny Lind in Donizetti's *La Figlia del Regimento*.

5   Arranges the lease of a house at Shepherd's Bush, financed by Miss Coutts as a refuge for homeless women (see ?13 Nov).

8–12   Acts as a mediator in a quarrel between JF and Thackeray.

11   Takes Haldimand on a visit to the Tothill Fields House of Correction.

13   The tenth number of *D&S* is 'not yet begun' (to Macready).

19   Tells Thompson that 'Between Dombey and Management I am one half mad and the other half addled' (the managerial responsibilities are related to theatricals: see 26 July below). A similar complaint has been made to G. H. Lewes four days earlier.

21   Gives a dinner-party for JF, Macready, Tom Taylor, Thackeray and others.

28   The Dickens family go to Broadstairs and remain there until 27 September, CD visiting London frequently during this period for rehearsals and other business.

29   Reports to Thomas Curry that all the children are suffering from whooping-cough.

July

16   (Fri) Dines at Gore House. Rehearsal at Miss Kelly's Theatre, 73

Dean Street; further rehearsals every evening in the following
week. CD stays at Victoria Hotel, Euston Square.

24   Dines with Jerrold; other guests include JF, Leigh Hunt, Maclise
and Macready.

25   The company of players travels to Manchester, Catherine and
Georgina accompanying CD.

26   They perform *Every Man in his Humour*, CD again playing
Bobadil, and two farces, Gore's *A Good Night's Rest* and Poole's
Turning the Tables.

27   They travel to Liverpool, and that evening CD attends a soirée
and dances 'like a madman' (to Mitton 8 Aug).

28   They perform Jonson's comedy and Peake's *Comfortable
Lodgings* in Liverpool. In both Manchester and Liverpool, CD is
given a very enthusiastic reception, the audiences 'standing up
as one person, and shouting incessantly for a good ten minutes'
(to Mitton, 8 Aug). These performances, and similar ones in
London, were originally planned to raise money for Leigh
Hunt; but, when Hunt learned on 24 June that he had been
granted a Civil List pension, the London performances were
cancelled and it was decided to divide the proceeds of the
northern performances between Hunt and John Poole.

August

1   (Sun) CD returns to Broadstairs.

4   Tells JF that he is thinking of writing a comic account of the
recent tour 'in the character of Mrs Gamp', to be published with
illustrations in order to raise a further sum for Hunt and Poole.
The possible titles proposed are 'The New Piljan's Projiss', 'Mrs
Gamp's Vacation' and 'Mrs Gamp in the Provinces'. CD reports
the work to Lewes a week later as 'nearly done', and JF quotes
the opening section of it in his *Life*; but it was never completed,
and the manuscript is lost.

17   Tells Miss Coutts that he is seriously behind-hand with the
current number (the twelfth) of *D&S*.

22   Goes to London for a few days and is able to move back into 1
Devonshire Terrace, his tenant having at last moved out and
some redecorations having been completed.

26   Sees *Cymbeline* at Sadler's Wells with JF.

28   Returns to Broadstairs, accompanied by Frank Stone.

30   Hans Andersen dines with the Dickens family.

31   CD goes to Ramsgate to say goodbye to Andersen, who is

embarking for Ostend. He takes Frank Stone on a seventeen-mile walk. He writes to Frank Duncker that a Christmas book this year is 'most probable' (but see 12 Sep).

September
1 (Wed) Visits Canterbury.
8 Goes to see *As You Like It* at Margate Theatre.
10 Beard arrives in Broadstairs to spend the weekend.
12 Sends to JF the opening portion of *The Haunted Man*. In the event, on account of his difficulties with *D&S*, he abandons the idea of completing it in time for Christmas, and it does not appear until the following year.
19 Tells JF, whom he also consults on the question of postponing *The Haunted Man*, that he has been 'at work all day' on the thirteenth number of *D&S*.
27 Leaves Broadstairs and visits Maidstone.
28 Visits Rochester.
?29 Returns to London.

October
12 (Tues) Tells Frederick Dickens that his engagement to Anne Weller is 'one of the greatest mistakes that ever was made'.
16 Dines with Macready; JF is among the other guests.
19 Attends a reading by Macready of Sir Henry Taylor's drama *Philip Van Artevelde*. Among others present are JF, Stanfield and Taylor (see also 22 Nov).

November
?13 (Sat) The 'home for homeless women' at Shepherd's Bush, soon to be named Urania Cottage, on which CD has expended much time and energy on Miss Coutts's behalf during the preceding months, is officially opened.
22 Goes with JF, Maclise, Stanfield and other friends to see Macready in *Philip Van Artevelde* (see 19 Oct), and the next day writes very warmly to Macready concerning his admiration and friendship.
23 Tells Macready that he is 'in the whirlwind of finishing a Number with a Crisis in it' – i.e. the fifteenth number of *D&S*, in which Florence Dombey flees from her home.
27 Goes to stay with the Watsons at Rockingham Castle, Northamptonshire (until 3 Dec).

December

1	(Wed) Presides at a soirée of the Leeds Mechanics' Institution and the next day tells JF 'I think I never did better'.

2	Reads the sixteenth number of *D&S* at Rockingham Castle.

3	Returns to London.

9	The Watsons and Fonblanque dine with CD.

21	Receives a letter from Jeffrey, who states that he refuses to believe that Edith Dombey is Carker's mistress. This prompts CD to ask JF's opinion of a change of intention involving 'a tremendous scene of her undeceiving Carker, and giving him to know that she never meant that'.

23	Finishes the sixteenth number of *D&S*.

27	Travels with Catherine to Edinburgh (Royal Hotel).

28	They proceed to Glasgow. Between Edinburgh and Glasgow, Catherine has a miscarriage in the train. In Glasgow they spend two nights with Sir Archibald Alison at Possil House, and Catherine is attended by Professor James Simpson, from whom CD learns about the use of chloroform (see also 16 Jan 1849). CD speaks at a soirée of the Athenaeum held at Glasgow City Hall.

29	CD and Alison visit Glasgow Royal Lunatic Asylum and a prison. CD is entertained to lunch by the Lord Provost.

30	CD and Catherine return to Edinburgh, where they stay with Jeffrey until 2 January.

31	Sixteenth number of *D&S* is published, and Jeffrey weeps over 'the little loves of Florence and Walter' (CD to Miss Coutts, ?4 Jan 1848).

1848

January

3	(Mon) CD and Catherine return to London from Scotland.

5	Catherine is still 'very unwell' (to Dr Alison) after her miscarriage (see 28 Dec 1847); five days later CD reports her recovery to Mark Lemon.

6	The Dickens family give their customary Twelfth Night party.

10	CD is 'trying to begin' the seventeenth number of *D&S* (to Lemon).

13	Visits Urania Cottage (and again on the 15th and 28th).

24	Dines with JF at Jack Straw's Castle, and discusses the proofs of the seventeenth number of *D&S*.

February

8 (Thurs) Visits Urania Cottage.

17 Is 'deep in No. 18' of *D&S*, in which Carker's flight and death occur. (To the Revd Edward Tagart, whom he also informs that 'Dombey flourishes exceedingly' – i.e. with respect to sales. Sales of the first four numbers have reached 122,035 by the end of 1847. It maintains its sales in the coming months; the press run rises to 33,000 after little Paul's death in the fifth number and reaches 35,000 by the end of serialisation.)

26 Publishes a review of Catherine Crowe's *The Night Side of Nature* in *The Examiner*.

29 Goes to Brighton with Catherine and Mrs Macready, in order to finish *D&S*. They stay first at the Bedford Hotel, then at 5 Junction House.

March

6 (Mon) Goes to London on business.

7 Visits Urania Cottage. Later in the week he returns to Brighton.

15 Tells Fanny Kelly that he has been 'working so hard [at *D&S*] that I have scarcely written any letters this fortnight past'.

16 In London again.

21 *D&S* 'not yet finished' (to Miss Coutts), but evidently finishes it in the next two or three days.

24 Writes the preface to *D&S*.

25 Tells JF to add to the proofs of *D&S* a reference to Diogenes, Florence Dombey's dog, which has been overlooked in the final round-up of characters.

27–8 Visits Salisbury (spending the night of the 27th at the White Hart Hotel), Stonehenge and Marlborough, in the company of JF, Leech and Lemon.

31 Final double number of *D&S* is published. Visits Urania Cottage.

April

11 (Tues) Gives a dinner at 1 Devonshire Terrace to celebrate the completion of *D&S*: the guests include Ainsworth, Beard, Browne, Burnett, D'Orsay, Evans, JF, Hogarth, Jerdan, Lemon, Macready and Stone.

12 Publication of *D&S* in volume form.

14 At work on an article, 'Ignorance and its Victims', published in *The Examiner* on the 22nd.

17 Speaks at the annual dinner of the General Theatrical Fund.
18 Visits Urania Cottage.
20 Purchases £600 worth of Consols, 'the first of many such investments that appear in the Coutts records from this time forward' (Patten, *CD and his Publishers*, p. 186).
21 Finishes reading JF's biography of Goldsmith (published 15 Apr).
22 Rehearsal at Miss Kelly's theatre (see May).
29 Attends the annual dinner of the Royal Academy with Macready.

May
In the early part of the month, CD is busy with rehearsals for the performances on the 15th and 17th. Later in the month, he is occupied with plans for the provincial performances in June, and reports himself to Lemon on the 22nd as 'up to the eyes' in correspondence relating to the tour.
7 (Sun) CD notes in a letter to JF that it is the eleventh anniversary of Mary Hogarth's death.
15 CD and friends perform Shakespeare's *The Merry Wives of Windsor* (with CD as Shallow) at the Haymarket Theatre, followed by Mrs Inchbald's farce *Animal Magnetism*.
17 They perform Jonson's *Every Man in his Humour* (with CD as Bobadil) and James Kenney's *Love, Law and Physic* at the Haymarket. The profits of these two performances go towards the endowment of a curatorship for Shakespeare's house at Stratford, the curator to be a distinguished author and preferably a dramatist, and Sheridan Knowles being intended as the first holder of the post.
23 The amateur players hold a reunion dinner at the Crown and Sceptre, Greenwich.
24 CD attends an evening party at Macready's; other guests include Ainsworth and Rogers.
25 Goes with Talfourd to a Shakespearean reading by Fanny Kelly.
26 CD and Catherine go to Birmingham (Royal Hotel) in connection with arrangements for the performance there.
28 They travel from Birmingham to Liverpool, and stay at Seaforth Hall as the guests of James Muspratt.
30 They go to Manchester.
31 They return to London, CD now suffering from a very heavy cold.

June

3   (Sat) The amateur players perform the *Merry Wives* in Manchester.

5   They perform the same play in Liverpool.

6   They leave Liverpool in the morning, rehearse Jonson's comedy at Birmingham in the afternoon, and perform it in the evening.

7   CD, accompanied by Georgina, Frederick Dickens, Egg, Lemon, Lewes and Stone, visits Stratford.

13   Dines with Macready.

24   CD's current account at Coutts's Bank now stands at £1937 17s. 10d.

26   Goes to Birmingham (Dee's Royal Hotel).

27   The amateur players perform the *Merry Wives* in Birmingham. Plans to perform also in Bristol and Plymouth fail to materialise (see July for performances in Scotland).

July

In the early part of the month, preparations for the performances in Scotland occupy much of CD's time.

1   (Sat) Visits Urania Cottage.

5   Visits his sister Fanny, who is dying of consumption.

7   Rehearsal at Miss Kelly's theatre.

10   Attends Macready's benefit performance at Drury Lane, which is also attended by the Queen and Prince Consort.

15   CD and his fellow-actors leave by train for Edinburgh.

17   They perform at Edinburgh.

18   They proceed to Glasgow and perform there in the evening.

20   Second performance at Glasgow, after which they return to London.

29   CD and Catherine go to Broadstairs, Georgina and the children having gone there a few days earlier.

August

In Broadstairs for this month; but as usual CD makes frequent visits to London.

9   (Wed) Catherine is involved in an accident while riding in a pony-chaise, and is slightly injured.

September

In Broadstairs for most of the month, with periodic visits to London.

1 (Fri) CD returns to London and visits his dying sister at Hornsey.

2 Death of Fanny Burnett, sister of CD. He goes to Broadstairs to escort Catherine back to London for the funeral.

6 Dines with Macready, who is leaving for America.

8 Attends Fanny's funeral at Highgate Cemetery.

9 Returns to Broadstairs.

30 Leaves Broadstairs and, *en route* for London, visits Maidstone, Rochester and Cobham in the course of a short walking-tour with JF and Stone.

October

3 (Tues) Arrives back in London.

4 Visits Urania Cottage

5 Tells Dr James Kay-Shuttleworth that he intends to write 'a little Christmas book' – i.e. *The Haunted Man*; the letter states that it is not yet begun, but on the same day he tells the Hon. Mrs Richard Watson that he 'entered on the first stage of its composition this morning, which is sitting frowning horribly at a quire of paper'.

20 Invests £2000 in 3¼ per cent Consols.

27 Goes with Leech to the Britannia Saloon (theatre), where one of the attractions is a man with a wooden leg dancing the Highland fling.

30 John Tenniel, one of the illustrators for *The Haunted Man*, visits CD.

November

10 (Fri) Mark Lemon visits CD.

13 CD suggests to JF that they and other friends should visit the Isle of Wight; the idea is later abandoned and a visit made instead to Norfolk (see 31 Dec, and 7 Jan 1849).

18 CD sees Stanfield, another of the illustrators for *The Haunted Man*.

19 Is engaged in finishing the second chapter of *The Haunted Man*.

22 Goes to Brighton (Bedford Hotel), presumably in order to finish his Christmas book.

30 Finishes *The Haunted Man*, 'having been crying my eyes out over it . . . these last three days' (to William Bradbury, 1 Dec).

December

Returns to London from Brighton at the beginning of the month.

5   (Tues) CD's brother Augustus marries Harriet Lovell at Trinity
    Church, Marylebone; the wedding-breakfast is held at CD's
    home.
7   Writes a review of Robert Hunt's *The Poetry of Science* for *The
    Examiner* (published 9 Dec).
11 Chapman, Miss Coutts, JF, Stanfield and the Watsons dine
    with CD, who after dinner reads *The Haunted Man*.
12 Dines with Miss Coutts; Rogers and the Watsons are among
    those present.
19 Publication of *The Haunted Man*. On the evening of the same
    day, a dramatisation opens at the Adelphi Theatre (running
    until 7 Feb); CD attends rehearsals on this and the previous
    day. He tells Thomas Beard that the book has sold 18,000 copies
    on the day of publication.
31 CD suggests Norwich and Stanfield Hall, near Wymondham,
    Norfolk, as destinations for the holiday trip with JF and others
    (see 13 Nov).

1849

January
2   (Tues) CD has supper with Mark Lemon.
3   Dinner at 1 Devonshire Terrace to celebrate the success of *The
    Haunted Man*; the guests include Bradbury, Evans, JF, Leech,
    Lemon, Stanfield, Stone and Tenniel.
6   The customary party to celebrate Twelfth Night and Charley's
    birthday: CD once more performs conjuring-tricks; he also
    dances with Mrs Macready for 'two mortal hours' (to Macready,
    2 Feb). During the previous night, he has jumped out of bed in
    order to practise the polka.
7   Sets out for a short holiday with Leech and Lemon. They travel
    by train to Norwich, where they spend the first night.
8   They view Norwich Cathedral; then ride to Stanfield Hall,
    scene of a celebrated recent double murder, and proceed to
    Yarmouth, where they spend two nights at the Royal Hotel.
9   They walk from Yarmouth to Lowestoft and back; on the way
    CD sees on a signpost the name Blundeston (a village off the
    main road), later used (as 'Blunderstone') in *David Copperfield*.
10 They return to London via Cambridge.
16 Birth of Henry Fielding Dickens, eighth child of CD; five days

later CD tells William Empson that 'Chloroform did wonders' (for his introduction to the possibilities of chloroform, see 28 Dec 1847).

20 CD publishes the first of three articles in *The Examiner* on the Tooting baby-farm scandal (others on 27 Jan and 21 April). JF's diary entry for this date refers to the manuscript of CD's fragment of autobiography, perhaps written in 1845 or 1846, which is to form the basis for portions of the early chapters of *DC*.

29 Death of Henry (Harry) Burnett, CD's crippled nephew, aged nine.

31 CD goes to Lewisham to visit his father, who is unwell.

February

1 (Thurs) Goes to Lewisham again (see previous day).

3 Tells Henry Austin that he is 'revolving a new work'. Visits Urania Cottage.

5 Attends the funeral of Harry Burnett.

7 CD's thirty-seventh birthday: Beard, JF and Stone dine at his home.

8 Visits Henry Austin at Brighton.

10 Visits Urania Cottage.

14 After doing business with Bradbury and Evans and then at the offices of the Royal Literary Fund, CD travels by train to Brighton, where he and Catherine and the Leeches stay at Junction House.

17 In the evening, after the landlord and his daughter have both gone 'raving mad', the party move to the Bedford Hotel.

?18 'My mind running, like a high sea, on names [for *DC*] – not satisfied yet, though' (to JF).

20 Declines an invitation to stand as candidate for the Rectorship of Marischal College, Aberdeen.

21 Returns to London.

26 Sends to JF a list of possible titles for the new novel.

27 Tells Miss Coutts that he is 'in the first agonies of a new book'.

March

?5 (Mon) Tells JF that he is at work on *DC*.

16 Tells Lemon that he has been 'at work all day'.

24 Tells Miss Coutts that he is working hard to finish the first

number (chs 1–3) of *DC*. In the evening, he gives a large dinner-party.

26 Goes with Leech, Lemon and Stone – who, with CD, constitute the 'Walking Club' and meet weekly – to Slough by train and thence for a ramble.

April

?19 (Thurs) Tells JF that he is having difficulties with *DC* and has written nothing for two days.

30 First number of *DC* is published; monthly instalments continue until 31 October 1850.

May

5 (Sat) Sends the final portion of the manuscript of the second number of *DC* (chs 4–6) to Evans, his publisher.

6 Goes to Gore House, where the contents are on view preceding their sale by action (Lady Blessington and Count D'Orsay have fled to Paris in the previous month in order to escape their creditors).

12 Gives a dinner to celebrate the launching of *DC* at which the guests include Browne, the Carlyles, JF, Mrs Gaskell, Jerrold and Rogers; Thackeray and others join them after dinner.

14 Dines with Mrs Gaskell and then goes with her to Drury Lane to see Weber's opera *Der Freischütz*.

21 Speaks at the annual dinner of the General Theatrical Fund.

23 Goes to the Derby with Leech, Lemon and John Gordon; the experience is later drawn on in CD's *HW* article 'Epsom', written jointly with Wills and published on 7 June 1851.

28–9 CD and Catherine are the guests of Lord Nugent at Lilies near Aylesbury.

June

4 (Mon) Death of Lady Blessington.

6 CD tells JF that the current number of *DC* (the third) is half finished, and that he has a 'move' (an idea for the development of the story) in mind for this and the next two numbers.

14 Goes to the Hampton Races with Leech.

16 Visits Cobham with Leech and Stone.

15 Visits Urania Cottage.

19 Speaks at a dinner of the United Law Clerks' Society.

20 Attends a charity fete in Holland Park held by the Scottish Society of London.
21 Takes a country walk of fourteen miles, 'revolving number four!' (to JF). The third number of DC (chs 7–9) has evidently been completed by this date.
30 Visits Urania Cottage.

July
1 (Sun) Has a fall that leaves him unwell for a few days.
2 Visits Urania Cottage.
?3 Goes to see Donizetti's *Lucrezia Borgia* at Her Majesty's Theatre.
4 Sends the manuscript of the first part of the fourth number of DC to Evans.
7 Speaks at a Mansion House banquet.
8 Goes to Broadstairs (until the 14th) to recuperate from the effects of his fall (see 1 July above), and to finish the fourth number (chs 10–12) of DC.
15 Leaves London with Leech for the Isle of Wight.
16 Tells Catherine that he has rented Winterbourne Villa (now Winterbourne Hotel), a house at Bonchurch, Isle of Wight, as a holiday home.
17 Returns to London.
26 Goes to Bonchurch with his family for their summer holiday (until 1 Oct),
28 In a letter to Bradbury, CD refers to the idea of a weekly magazine to be published under his editorship.

August
1 (Wed) CD settles down to work at Bonchurch on the fifth number (chs 13–15) of DC; a few days later he describes himself, in letters to JF and Miss Coutts, as working at it, and also mentions to JF his habit of working in the mornings and making himself 'invisible' until 2 p.m. each day during family holidays.

September
The Dickens family remain at Bonchurch during this month, and CD is visited by a number of his relatives and friends, including Beard, Leech and Stone. Leech falls ill in the latter part of the month and is 'magnetized' (hypnotised) by CD.
?18 (Tues) Finishes the sixth number (chs 16–18) of DC.
24 'The old notion of the Periodical, which has been agitating itself

in my mind for so long, I really think is at last gradually growing into form' (to JF).

October
1   (Mon) Returns to London, then (with Catherine, Georgina and the two girls) goes on to Broadstairs (until the 18th).
4   Visits Canterbury.
7   Writes to JF about the idea of a weekly magazine.
18 Returns to London.
27 Publishes an Article, 'Macready as King Lear', in *The Examiner*.

November
5   (Mon) Gives a dinner for the Watsons, who are visiting London.
6   Attends a committee meeting at Urania Cottage.
10 Attends a party at Talfourd's.
13 With JF, Leech and other friends, CD watches the public execution of the Mannings – the first execution of a married couple since 1700 – from the roof of a house facing Horsemonger Lane Gaol. *The Times* later reports that a crowd of over 30,000 is present. CD then writes a letter to *The Times*, published the next day, concerning public executions.
17 Writes again to *The Times* on the same subject (letter published on the 18th). The two letters are published as a pamphlet later in the year.
20 Tells JF that the current number (8) of *DC* has been completed 'after two days' very hard work indeed', and describes it as 'a smashing number'.
21 Speaks at a dinner of the Newsvendors' Benevolent Institution.
26 The Dickens family go to Rockingham Castle, Northamptonshire, to stay with the Watsons (until the 30th). CD meets Mary Boyle, who is also a guest.
29 CD and Mary Boyle perform scenes from Sheridan's *The School for Scandal* and a dramatisation of *NN* as part of an after-dinner entertainment; CD also performs conjuring-tricks.

December
1   (Sat) CD visits Eton College in connection with Charley's entry.
4   Dines with Macready; the other guests include Elliotson, JF, Jerrold and Stanfield.

9   Goes to the Adelphi Theatre to see Boucicault and Kenney's *The Willow Copse* and other pieces.
18   Receives a letter from Mrs Seymour Hill, complaining that he has used her as a model for Miss Mowcher in *DC*; he replies at once, assuring her that he will modify his plans for this character. He also (20–1 Dec) exchanges letters with her solicitor.
22   Visits Urania Cottage.

1850

January
During this month, CD tries out on JF more than a dozen possible titles for his new weekly magazine, and finally settles on *Household Words*.
23   (Wed) Tells JF that he feels 'a great hope that I shall be remembered by little Em'ly, a good many years to come'.
28   Hears that Jeffrey has died on the 26th, and is 'stunned by the announcement': 'he was a most affectionate and devoted friend to me' (to JF, 29 Jan).
31   Invites Mrs Gaskell to contribute 'a short tale, or any number of tales' to *HW* (*Lizzie Leigh* is serialised in the first three issues).

February
6   (Wed) Speaks at a dinner of the Metropolitan Sanitary Association.
20   'Copperfield runs high, and must be done to-morrow' (to JF) – that is, he plans to complete the eleventh number by the 21st.

March
4   (Mon) Invites Tom Taylor to contribute to *HW*.
7   Goes to Brighton 'to pursue Copperfield in peace' (to Miss Coutts, 6 Mar).
14   Sends to JF the manuscript of 'A Child's Dream of a Star' (published in the second issue of *HW*), the idea for which he has conceived 'as I was coming down [to Brighton] in the railroad the other night'. Tells Bradbury that the first issue of *HW* is 'an extraordinary production, and if the Public are not satisfied, I don't know what they would have'.

25   Speaks at the annual dinner of the General Theatrical Fund.
30   The first issue of *HW* is published; the magazine continues
     weekly until 28 May 1859.

April
12   (Fri) Tells Miss Coutts that *HW* is 'exceedingly well liked, and
     "goes" in the trade phrase admirably'.
During the month *The Household Narrative of Current Events*, a
monthly news supplement to *HW*, begins publication, continuing
to the end of 1855.

May
 7   (Tues) Tells JF that he has 'begun Copperfield [i.e. the
     fourteenth number] this morning' and is 'still undecided about
     Dora, but MUST decide to-day' (the number includes David's
     engagement and marriage to Dora).

June
11   (Tues) Tells Macready, 'Between Copperfield and Household
     Words I am as busy as a bee.'
20   Dines with Macready; JF and Talfourd are also present.
Towards the end of the month, CD goes to Paris with Maclise for
a short holiday; he stays at the Hotel Windsor, attends various
theatres, including a performance by Rachel on the 26th, and visits
Lord Normanby (British Ambassador), John Poole and others.

July
 3   (Wed) Begs Mrs Gaskell to let him have another story for *HW*.
     The sudden death of Sir Robert Peel on the previous day is a
     considerable shock to him.

August
 1   (Thurs) Describes (in a letter to Miss Coutts) a visit to the
     Westminster Ragged School.
16   Birth of Dora Annie, ninth child of CD. After Catherine's
     confinement, he goes to Broadstairs, where the other children
     have already been installed at Fort House. He remains there,
     with frequent visits to London, until 28 October.
20   'I have been very hard at work [on the seventeenth number of
     DC] these three days, and have still Dora to kill' (Dora dies in
     ch. 53, the last of the three chapters comprising this number),

September
2 (Mon) Walks from Broadstairs to Richborough Castle and back with Charles Knight, JF and Charley Dickens.
6 Catherine joins her family at Broadstairs.
15 Tells JF that he has been 'tremendously at work these two days [on the eighteenth number of *DC*]; eight hours at a stretch yesterday, and six hours and a half to-day, with the Ham and Steerforth chapter [ch. 55, the second of the four chapters comprising this number]'.
22 Tells Miss Coutts that he will soon be 'sitting down to my final wrestle with Copperfield' – i.e. the final double number.

October
During this month, plans for a performance of *Every Man in his Humour* at Knebworth, Bulwer-Lytton's country house in Hertfordshire, which have begun to take shape in September, are pursued (see 18–20 Nov).
21 (Mon) Tells JF that he is 'within three pages' of the end of *DC*, and is 'strongly divided, as usual in such cases, between sorrow and joy'.
23 Sends the final chapter of *DC*, with the Preface, to Evans.
24 Dines with JF; Macready and Maclise are also present.
28 The Dickens family return to London from Broadstairs.
31 Rehearsal of *Every Man in his Humour* at Miss Kelly's theatre (and another on 1 Nov).

November
Theatricals occupy much of CD's time and energies during this month: on the 3rd he tells Bulwer-Lytton to regard him as 'wholly at the disposal of the Theatricals until they shall be gloriously achieved'.
14 (Thurs) Goes to Knebworth.
18–20 Three performances of Jonson's comedy take place at Knebworth; everything goes off 'in a whirl of triumph' (to the Hon. Mrs Watson, 23 Nov). CD's fellow actors include JF, Leech, Lemon, Jerrold, Stone, Georgina Hogarth; Catherine Dickens drops out of the cast on account of illness, and Mary Boyle on account of a bereavement.

December
During the first few days of the month, CD is 'so very unwell . . .

that I have hardly been able to hold up my head' (to Landor, 4 Dec).

 3 (Tues) JF and Macready dine with CD, who is 'not well' (Macready's diary).

 8 Bulwer-Lytton, JF, Jerrold and Macready dine with CD.

11 The Watsons dine with CD.

15 JF, Macready, Sir Joseph Paxton and others dine with CD.

19 Attends an evening party at Talfourd's; others present include JF, Maclise, Macready and the Procters.

23 Visits the Watsons at Rockingham in connection with arrangements for further theatricals (see next month), and returns to London the same day.

1851

January
 1 (Wed) Tells Bulwer-Lytton that he finds his comedy *Not So Bad as we Seem 'most admirable'* and *'certain to go nobly'* (see 16 May).

 5 Refers (in a letter to Bulwer-Lytton) to the scheme to establish the Guild of Literature and Art, evidently discussed when he was at Knebworth (see Nov 1850). The plan is to raise money by performances of Lytton's comedy (see previous entry) in London and the provinces.

 8 CD travels to Rockingham to begin a week of preparations and rehearsals.

15 Performance at Rockingham of *A Day after the Wedding, Used Up* and *Animal Magnetism*.

16 Leaves Rockingham.

25 Tells Leech that he is thinking of going to Paris 'for a purpose'.

February
 3 (Mon) Attends the Haymarket Theatre to see Macready in *King Lear*. Leech and his wife accompany CD, but Catherine and Georgina stay at home on account of the serious illness of the baby, Dora.

10 Goes to Paris with Leech and Spencer Lyttelton; they cross by the Boulogne mail-boat and stay at the Hotel Wagram.

12 D'Orsay dines with CD, who returns the visit the next day. CD also meets Lord and Lady Castlereagh.

13 CD and Leech take a long early morning walk and then have breakfast at Poissy.

14   They leave Paris to travel to London via Calais, and arrive home
     on the next day.
18   Death of George Thomson, grandfather of Catherine Dickens.
26   CD attends Drury Lane Theatre to see Macready as Macbeth –
     his final appearance.

March
During this month CD is much occupied with plans for the
performance before the Queen at Devonshire House; on the 23rd he
tells Bulwer-Lytton that 'the amount of business and
correspondence . . . is about (I should imagine) equal to the
business of the Home Office'.
 1   (Sat) Proposes Macready's health at a farewell dinner given to
     the actor at the London Tavern; Bulwer-Lytton is in the chair.
 8   Tells Dr James Wilson of Malvern that he is 'anxious to place
     Mrs Dickens under your care', her case being 'a nervous one
     . . . of a peculiar kind'.
13   Accompanies Catherine to Malvern, where Georgina remains
     with her in lodgings (Knutsford Lodge); the children remain in
     London. Catherine takes the cold-water cure, and CD spends
     several weeks in Malvern with frequent visits to London on
     business and for rehearsals.
20   CD makes an offer of £2700 for Balmoral House, owned by
     William Booth and overlooking Regent's Park; the offer is not
     accepted.
24–5 Rehearsals held at Covent Garden.
?25 John Dickens undergoes surgery.
27   CD visits his father twice.
28   Reports his father as 'very dangerously ill' (to Mitton).
31   Death of John Dickens at 5.35 a.m. CD has arrived at 34 Keppel
     Street from Malvern at 11.15 p.m. on the previous night, and is
     with him when he dies.

April
 5   (Sat) Attends funeral of John Dickens at Highgate Cemetery.
14   Presides at the annual dinner of the General Theatrical Fund.
     After it is concluded, CD learns that his baby daughter Dora has
     died, aged not quite eight months. (A letter written the next day
     states that his servant broke the news, but according to JF the
     servant told him and he communicated it to CD with the
     assistance of Lemon.)

15 Writes to Catherine, who is still in Malvern, breaking the news of Dora's death. JF takes the letter to Malvern and accompanies her and Georgina to London, leaving Lemon to spend the night with CD sitting beside the child's body. CD postpones the performance of the play that has been arranged for 30 April.

19 Tells Beard that Catherine is 'very low', and describes himself to Mitton as 'quite happy again', adding that he has 'undergone a good deal'.

May

1 (Thurs) At work on the farce *Mr Nightingale's Diary*. The Great Exhibition opens in Hyde Park (see 11 July).

3 Speaks at the Royal Academy banquet.

10 Speaks at a dinner of the Metropolitan Sanitary Association held at Gore House.

14 Dress rehearsal at Devonshire House.

16 Performance at Devonshire House of Bulwer-Lytton's *Not So Bad as we Seem* before the Queen and the Prince Consort, in aid of the Guild of Literature and Art. CD plays the role of Lord Wilmot, and the cast also includes Wilkie Collins, Egg, JF, Horne, Jerrold, Knight, Lemon, Stone and Tenniel – 'The whole produced under the direction of Mr Charles Dickens' (playbill).

27 At the Duke of Devonshire's request, the play is repeated at Devonshire House, this time with the farce *Mr Nightingale's Diary*, in which CD plays six parts. Afterwards the Duke gives a ball and supper for the actors.

June

The Dickens home at 1 Devonshire Terrace is let for the summer, the family moving to Fort House, Broadstairs. CD spends much of his time in London, sleeping at the *HW* office in Wellington Street, where he has a flat.

9 (Mon) Speaks at a dinner of the Gardeners' Benevolent Institution.

18 and 21 The comedy and farce are repeated at the Hanover Square Rooms.

23 Visits Macready's home in Dorset (Sherborne House) for a few days.

July

1 (Tues) CD takes Charley and three of his Eton friends for an

excursion on the Thames; Thomas Beard, Charley's godfather, accompanies him.

11   Tells the Hon. Mrs Watson that he has been twice to the Great Exhibition.

20   Authorises Frank Stone to offer £1450 on his behalf for Tavistock House, Tavistock Square; the offer is accepted.

During this month he reads 'that wonderful book', Carlyle's *The French Revolution*, 'for the 500th time' (to JF); also Hawthorne's *The Scarlet Letter*, which he finds 'falls off sadly after that fine opening scene'.

August

17   (Sun) 'I begin to be pondering afar off, a new book. Violent restlessness and vague ideas of going I don't know where, I don't know why' (to Miss Coutts). At about the same time he tells JF that he is 'the victim of an intolerable restlessness'.

September

During this and the next two months, CD is much preoccupied with arrangements for the move to Tavistock House, where extensive renovations and redecorations are being carried out.

7   (Sun) Tells Henry Austin that his next book is 'waiting to be born'.

October

6   (Mon) Tells Beard that he is 'wild to begin a new book'. During this month Bradbury and Evans announce 'a new serial work' by CD.

20   The Dickens family return to London from Broadstairs.

November

11   (Tues) Performance of *Not So Bad as we Seem* and *Mr Nightingale's Diary* at Bath. While in that city, CD calls on Landor.

12   Performance at Clifton, where the enthusiasm of the audience is 'prodigious' (to Catherine, 13 Nov). The performance is repeated on the 14th.

By the end of this month, the move to Tavistock House has been completed.

December
4 (Fri) Knight and the Watsons dine with CD.
7 CD has only one more short chapter to write in order to complete the opening number of his new novel (*Bleak House*).
9 Performance at Reading.
26 Visits St Luke's Hospital for the Insane in order to observe the Christmas festivities there (see 'A Curious Dance round a Curious Tree', *HW* 17 Jan 1852).
?30 Mrs Gaskell mentions in a letter that she has heard from a London informant that 'the Dickens have bought a dinner-service of *gold* plate'.

1852

January
7 (Wed) CD is ill with 'a most deplorable bilious cold' (to Benjamin Webster).
27 Declines an invitation from Mrs Gaskell because he is fully occupied with rehearsals, which are going ahead for the forthcoming provincial tour of the amateur players. In the evening, he speaks at a dinner of the Newsvendors' Benevolent Institution.

February
4 (Wed) Tells Bulwer Lytton that Jerrold has 'deserted' them – i.e. has quitted the cast at the last moment. His place is taken by Wilkie Collins.
6 Walks with Leech on the Sussex Downs, and afterwards dines with him at the Bedford Hotel, Brighton.
7 CD's fortieth birthday.
8 Offers to read the first number of *BH* to Miss Coutts before publication.
11 Performance of *Not So Bad as we Seem* at the Manchester Free Trade Hall.
12 To Liverpool, where the Mayor gives a dinner to the Guild at the Town Hall.
13 and 14 Performances at the Liverpool Philharmonic Hall.
15 Leaves Liverpool at 4 a.m., and on the same day writes to Bulwer Lytton referring to the 'triumph' they have enjoyed. The actors

have been invited to pay a return visit to Manchester (see 1
Sep), and the profit on the tour has been over £1000.

24 CD and Catherine, accompanied by Leech, visit Eton, where
Charley is a pupil at the College.

March

1 (Mon) CD gives a dinner at his home for the members of the
Guild. The first number of *BH* appears (continuing monthly to
Sep 1853).

2 Tells Miss Coutts that on the previous night extra copies of the
opening number of *BH* have been printed in order to cope with
the heavy demand.

4 Tells George Hogarth that *BH* is 'a great success' and 'blazing
away merrily'.

6 Visits Highgate Cemetery, where his daughter Dora and other
members of his family are buried.

7 Sends to JF the proofs of the second number of *BH*, and tells him
that the sales of the first number were '30,000 when I last
heard'. (The initial printing has been 25,000; by the end of June,
38,500 copies of this opening number have been sold.)

13 Birth of Edward Bulwer Lytton, tenth child of CD: 'a brilliant
boy of unheard-of dimensions' (to Wills).

17 Tells JF that he will 'soften down words here and there' in the
description of Skimpole in *BH*: he has evidently also consulted
B. W. Procter on the matter. The next day, he tells JF that he has
'gone over every part of it very carefully, and I think I have
made it much less like [Leigh Hunt]'; he has also changed
Skimpole's name from Leonard to Harold.

23 Dines with Wills; JF is also present.

31 With Wills and Mary Boyle, spends the night at Rockingham
Castle, and leaves for Birmingham the next morning.

April

At the beginning of the month, CD visits Birmingham and
Shrewsbury to make arrangements for the performances there in
May.

5 (Mon) Speaks at the annual dinner of the General Theatrical
Fund.

21 Lemon dines with CD.

May

4   (Tues) Presides at a meeting called by the publisher John Chapman to discuss 'the removal of the present trade restrictions on the commerce of literature'.

6   Bulwer Lytton dines with CD.

8   Tells Cerjat that *BH* is 'a most enormous success; all the prestige of Copperfield (which was very great) falling upon it, and raising its circulation above all my other books'. (*DC* had 'maintained a circulation of under 22,000' [Patten, *CD and his Publishers*, p. 224], but the initial press run of the second number of *BH* was 32,000 and that of the third number 34,000.)

10   The amateur players perform at Shrewsbury Music Hall.

11   They travel to Birmingham, where CD is joined by Catherine and Georgina.

12 and 13   The players perform at Birmingham Town Hall. On the morning of the 13th, CD, Collins, Egg, Lemon, Tenniel and the Watsons visit three Birmingham factories, 'seeing the processes at all the places' (Mrs Watson's diary).

June

10   (Thurs) Lemon and Watson dine with CD.

14   Presides at a dinner of the Gardeners' Benevolent Institution.

16   Visits St Albans Prison.

July

1   (Thurs) Spends the day at Eton, accompanied by Beard.

11   The Hon. Richard Watson dines with CD and is 'full of projects for future happiness' (to Wills, 1 Aug). Townshend is also present.

22   By this date the Dickens family are installed at 10 Camden Crescent, Dover, for their summer holidays. As usual, CD is frequently absent in London and elsewhere. Dover turns out to be 'too bandy (I mean musical, no reference to its legs)' and 'infinitely too genteel' for CD's taste (to Mary Boyle, 22 July).

27   Death of the Hon. Richard Watson after a few days' illness: 'I loved him as my heart, and cannot think of him without tears' (to Knight, 1 Aug).

August

4   (Wed) Death of Count D'Orsay.

22   CD leaves London for Nottingham.

23   The amateur players perform *Not So Bad as we Seem* at Nottingham.
24   CD walks from Nottingham to Derby.
25   They perform at Derby.
27   They perform at Newcastle. CD tells the Duke of Devonshire that they are doing 'wonderfully well' and that he believes that all their houses will be 'crammed'.
28   They perform at Sunderland, CD having walked there from Newcastle.
30   They perform at Sheffield.
31   CD speaks at a banquet given at the Manchester Athenaeum in honour of the Guild.

September
1   (Wed) They perform at Manchester, where they are watched by an audience of about 4000. CD has been persuaded by Mrs Gaskell not to repeat Bulwer-Lytton's comedy in Manchester, and *Used Up* and *Mr Nightingale's Diary* are performed instead.
2   CD speaks at the opening by the Queen of the Manchester Free Library; Bulwer-Lytton and Thackeray are also among the speakers.
3   The players perform at Liverpool.
18   Death of Mrs Macready.
23   CD tells Miss Coutts that the public 'seems to me to have gone mad about the funeral of the Duke of Wellington'. (The Duke had died on 14 Sep and was buried at St Paul's on 18 Nov; the crowd that watched the funeral procession was estimated at 1.5 million.) (See however, 4, 12 and 18 Nov.)

October
3   (Sun) The holiday at Dover coming to an end, the Dickens children return to London and CD and Catherine cross to Boulogne for a two-week visit, staying at the Hotel des Bains.

November
4   (Thurs) CD declines an invitation from the Dean of St Paul's to attend the funeral of the Duke of Wellington, having already accepted the Duke of Devonshire's invitation to watch the procession from Devonshire House (he has proposed to the Duke that he should bring along a party of eleven members of his family and friends).

 6   Suggests to Mrs Gaskell that she make some changes in her *The Old Nurse's Story*, intended for *HW*.
12   Asks permission from the Headmaster of Eton for Charley to join the party watching the Duke of Wellington's funeral.
18   Funeral of the Duke of Wellington.

December
 2   (Thurs) An outing to Brighton with Leech: they walk on the Downs and dine at the Bedford Hotel.
28   Attends an annual 'dinner for poor people' given by Miss Coutts.
29   Visits Urania Cottage.
Towards the end of the month, a crisis in the *HW* office is caused by Wills's suddenly losing his sight.

1853

January
 6   (Thurs) A dinner is given in CD's honour at the rooms of the Birmingham Fine Arts Association, as a token of the esteem of the people of that city, and he is presented with a salver and a diamond ring.

February
 7   (Mon) CD thanks Dr Elliotson for the loan of his 'remarkable and learned Lecture on Spontaneous Combustion'.
21   On account of Wills's illness (see the last entry for the previous year), CD is 'sitting (up to the neck) in a quagmire' of contributions to *HW* (to Mrs Gaskell).

March
 2   (Wed) Goes to Brighton for two weeks, Catherine and Georgina having already gone there. They stay at 1 Junction Parade. Charley is by this time on his way to Leipzig to study German.
22   Speaks at the annual dinner of the Royal General Theatrical Fund.

April
20   (Wed) Dines at Devonshire House.
30   Speaks at the Royal Academy banquet.

May
2 (Mon) Speaks at the Mansion House dinner and meets Harriet Beecher Stowe.
8 Discusses with Lemon and Miss Kelly plans for an 'informal benefit' on behalf of the latter (it is subsequently arranged for 16 June, then postponed indefinitely),
12 Dines with Cornelius Felton at the Trafalgar, Greenwich.
22 The Régniers dine at CD's home, and an experiment in spiritualism is conducted, with apparent success.

June
In the early part of the month, CD is ill and spends six days in bed, 'for the first time in my life' (as he tells Lady Eastlake); he later attributes this illness to 'an old afflicted KIDNEY, once the torment of my childhood, in which I took cold' (to Wilkie Collins, 30 June). He decides that he needs a complete change.
11 (Sat) He is 'now growing vigorous again' (to E. M. Ward, from Folkestone).
12 Crosses to Boulogne with Catherine and Georgina.
13 Moves into the Villa des Moulineaux, rue Beaurepaire, Boulogne, which he has leased.
18 Tells Wills that he has 'picked up in the most extraordinary manner' and that he is at work on the seventeenth number of *BH* 'with great ease'.
23 Finishes the seventeenth number of *BH*.
29 Tells Browne that he has made a complete recovery, and sends subjects for the illustrations in the eighteenth number of *BH*, also promising that the subjects for the final double number will be posted to Browne within a day or two.

July
24 (Sun) Tells Macready that he has been working hard at *BH* since arriving in Boulogne and, after a week's rest, is now setting to work to finish the final instalment of that novel.

August
5 (Fri) Tells Wills that he is 'just getting fairly into' the conclusion of *BH*.
25 Reads the final instalment of *BH* to his family, and afterwards tells the Hon. Mrs Watson that it made a 'great impression' on them.

27 Mentions to Miss Coutts a plan to give readings from *CC* at Birmingham for charity (see 27 Dec). He states that he has been 'very hard at work' since arriving in Boulogne, 'often getting up at daybreak to write through many hours' (to the Hon. Mrs Watson).

September
Early in the month, and again early in October, CD spends a few days in London, mainly on *HW* business; apart from these visits, residence in Boulogne continues during September.

21 (Wed) Tells the Hon. Mrs Watson that he is 'finishing The Child's History' and clearing up outstanding work on *HW* before setting out on a tour (*A Child's History of England* appears intermittently in *HW* from 25 Jan 1851 to 10 Dec 1853).

October
?10 (Mon) Accompanied by Wilkie Collins and Augustus Egg, CD sets off on a tour of France, Switzerland and Italy; his family return to London.

13 In Strasbourg (Hotel de Paris).

16 In Lausanne.

20 In Chamonix (Hotel de Londres), having travelled there 'over very bad roads' from Geneva (to Catherine).

21 Leaves Chamonix for Martigny.

23 Crosses the Simplon Pass.

24 Arrives in Milan (Hotel de la Ville).

26 Leaves Milan for Genoa, where, after a 31-hour journey, they stay at the Croce di Malta.

November
1 (Tues) Leaves Genoa for Naples by the P. & O. steamer *Valetta*.

4 Arrives in Naples (Hotel des Etrangers). While there, CD meets Layard, who joins the party for the ascent of Vesuvius. CD attends a performance of Verdi's *Il Trovatore* at the San Carlo Opera ('It seemed rubbish on the whole to me': to Georgina, 13 Nov).

13 In Rome (Hotel des Iles Britanniques).

18 Leaves Rome for Florence, a journey (by post) of 3½ days.

21 Arrives in Florence.

23 Leaves Florence for Padua, via Bologna and Ferrara, a journey of 28½ hours.

25 In Venice.

December
 5 (Mon) In Turin. Subsequently returns to England via Marseilles and Paris, crossing from Calais to Dover on the 11th.
27, 29 and 30 Gives three readings at the Birmingham Town Hall in aid of the Literary and Scientific Institute – his first public readings. (*CC* is read twice, and *The Cricket on the Hearth* on the 29th.)

1854

January
16 (Mon) Tells Cerjat that the strike at Preston, Lancashire, is still unsettled.
20 Sends to JF a list of fourteen possible titles for 'the Household Words story'.
23 Tells Miss Coutts that 'there is such a fixed idea on the part of my printers and co-partners in Household Words, that a story of me, continued from week to week, would make some unheard of effect with it, that I am going to write one': the outcome is *Hard Times*, intended to counteract the falling sales of the magazine.
28 In Preston to observe the effects of the strike; he stays at the Bull Hotel and visits the theatre, where he sees a bad performance of *Hamlet*.

February
 7 (Tues) CD's forty-second birthday is celebrated with a dinner at Waite's Hotel, Gravesend; among those present are Beard and Stanfield.
20 Asks Lemon for 'any slang terms [used] among the tumblers and circus-people that you can call to mind' (presumably for use in ch. 6 of *HT*).

March
 9 (Thurs) Dines with Charles Kemble.
10 Spends the day at Dover with Lemon.
13 Sudden death of Sir Thomas Talfourd; CD's tribute to 'this upright judge and good man' appears in *HW* on the 25th.

16 Spends the day at Ramsgate with Lemon.
17 Dines at Jack Straw's Castle with Lemon and Stanfield.
28 Crimean War begins.

April
 1 (Sat) Serialisation of *HT* begins in *HW*, continuing weekly to 12
    August.
 3 Spends the day in Kent, walking from Maidstone to Gravesend
    'through Cobham Woods' (to Miss Coutts, 31 Mar).
13 Agrees to become President of the Newsvendors' Benevolent
    and Provident Institution.
22 Presides at a dinner held at the Garrick Club to celebrate
    Shakespeare's birthday.
23 Goes to Folkestone to meet Georgina, who is returning from
    Boulogne, where she has presumably been making
    arrangements for the forthcoming holiday.

June
 1 (Thurs) Dines with the Revd W. Harness.
11 Walks on Hampstead Heath with Wilkie Collins, who
    afterwards dines at Tavistock House.
16 The Dickens family go to Boulogne for their annual holiday,
    staying at the Villa de Camp de Droite. Work on *HT* continues
    there.
During this month CD meets Edmund Yates.

July
12 (Wed) CD describes himself to Wilkie Collins as 'Bobbing up,
    corkwise, from a sea of Hard Times'.
13 Describes himself to Wills as 'stunned with work'. Asks
    Carlyle's permission to dedicate the volume edition of *HT* to
    him, and invites the Carlyles to spend a week at Boulogne in
    September.
14 Tells JF, 'I am three parts mad, and the fourth delirious, with
    perpetual rushing at Hard Times. I have done what I hope is a
    good thing with Stephen' – i.e. the account of his death in Book
    the Third, ch. 6.
17 Tells Wills that *HT* has been completed that morning.
18 Travels to London in order to deliver the final portion of *HT*.
20 Goes to the opera at Drury Lane with Miss Coutts; they see
    Donizetti's *Lucrezia Borgia*.

21　Dines at the Garrick Club with Beard.
24　Sits to the painter E. M. Ward in his study at Tavistock House. On this or the next day, he travels back to Boulogne.
26　Tells Mrs Gaskell that he will begin the publication of her novel *North and South* in *HW* at once; 'a NEW TALE by the author of Mary Barton' is announced in the issue of 30 July, and the novel is serialised from 2 September to 27 January 1855. (See also 14 Oct).
31　Tells Mrs Gaskell that he is 'so dreadfully lazy (after finishing Hard Times), and lie so much on the grass, reading books and going to sleep'.

August
During this and the next month, the Boulogne holiday continues. Even though *HT* is finished, however, CD is much occupied with editorial business in connection with *HW*. Wills visits Boulogne for a fortnight in September, and at other times they exchange 'a parcel every week' (to Mitton, 23 Sep). Each morning CD hears his son Frank read, 'generally with a very good effect on his tendency to stutter' (to the Revd M. Gibson, 3 Sep).

September
During this month, Mary Dickens, who has been seriously ill earlier in the year, falls ill with 'English cholera', but is fully recovered by the 21st.
20　(Wed) Dr Elliotson comes to dinner.
27　Beard arrives on a visit; Egg is also a visitor at this time, and Wilkie Collins has been there a little earlier.

October
　1　(Sun) Watches a military review at which Napoleon III is present.
11　Mitton arrives on a visit.
14　Tells Wills that he is 'not surprised' to hear that the sales of *HW* have fallen, since Mrs Gaskell's *North and South*, 'so divided, is wearisome in the last degree'.
17　The Dickens family return to London via Folkestone.

November
28　(Tues) Leigh Hunt and JF dine at Tavistock House. (CD usually dines with Wills at the *HW* office on Tuesdays, but this week does so on the Wednesday.)

December

7 (Thurs) Visits Rochester.
19 Gives a charity reading of *CC* at the Literary and Mechanics' Institution, Reading.
20 Visits Macready at his Dorset home and (21st) gives a charity reading at Sherborne.
24 Returns to London.
26 Reads to his children the Christmas play that he has written for them.
27 Goes to Bradford.
28 Gives a reading at St George's Hall, Bradford, in aid of the Educational Temperance Institute to an audience of 3700, returning to London later in the day.
30 Presides at a dinner of the Commercial Travellers' School.

1855

January

3 (Wed) CD tells Cerjat that Charley has returned to Germany and will embark on a business career; also that all nine children are 'well and happy'.
6 Dress rehearsal of the Christmas play at Tavistock House (see 26 Dec 1854): there have been rehearsals daily during the week, and the performance takes place on the 8th.
27 Goes to a pantomime at the Britannia Theatre with Lemon and Stanfield. Congratulates Mrs Gaskell on the conclusion of *North and South* as a serial in *HW*.

February

7 (Wed) CD's forty-third birthday is celebrated with a dinner at Gravesend; CD walks through heavy snow from Gravesend to Rochester. At Gravesend, he notices that Gad's Hill Place – 'literally "a dream of my childhood"' (to Wills, 9 Feb) – is for sale, and becomes interested in its purchase (see 24 Oct, and 9 Feb 1856).
9 Receives a letter from Mrs Maria Winter, née Beadnell: 'Three or four and twenty years vanished like a dream' (to Mrs Winter, 10 Feb). He writes again from Paris, and the correspondence continues; they meet soon after his return, to CD's abrupt and

bitter disillusionment, and the Winters subsequently dine at Tavistock House.

11 Sets off for Paris with Wilkie Collins; *en route* they spend the night in Boulogne, where two of CD's sons are at school.

12 Arrives in Paris, staying at the Hotel Meurice. During their stay, CD and Collins go to the theatre several times. A plan to extend the trip to Bordeaux is abandoned on account of bad weather (and perhaps also, as Michael Slater has suggested, because CD is impatient to see Mrs Winter).

?23 Returns to London.

March

3 (Sat) Goes to the Standard Theatre, Shoreditch, to see Miss Glyn in *Antony and Cleopatra*.

14 Attends the Annual General Meeting of the Royal Literary Fund.

23 Thanks Thackeray for his 'generous reference' to CD in the lecture on 'Charity and Humour' which he gave the previous evening at the Marylebone Institute, reported in this day's *Times* (CD is referred to in the lecture as 'a person commissioned by Divine Providence to correct and instruct his fellow-men').

27 Despite a cold, reads *CC* at Ashford, Kent, to an audience of railway workers; Lemon, Beard, Wills and Wilkie Collins accompany him and they all dine together before the performance.

April

2 (Mon) Speaks at a dinner of the Royal General Theatrical Fund.

20 Dines with Wilkie Collins.

26 Goes to Highgate Cemetery with Lemon, whose infant child has just died.

May

8 (Tues) Tells Miss Coutts that he is 'in a state of restlessness impossible to be described', and that he has 'a capital name' for his new novel (*Little Dorrit*).

10 Refers to increasing restlessness in another letter to Miss Coutts.

11 Tells Wilkie Collins that 'The restless condition in which I

wander up and down my room with the first page of my new book before me defies all description.'

12 Dines at Greenwich with Lemon.

20 Tells Stanfield that he is going to produce and act (with Lemon, Wilkie Collins, Egg and Mary Dickens) in a private performance of Collins's melodrama *The Lighthouse*.

21 Presides at a meeting of the Newsvendors' Benevolent Institution.

June

15 (Fri) Performance of *The Lighthouse* to an invited audience at Tavistock House: CD's farce *Mr Nightingale's Diary* is also staged.

16 Presides at a Special General Meeting of the Royal Literary Fund.

18–19 Two further performances take place.

27 Speaks at a meeting of the Administrative Reform Association.

July

3 (Tues) Calls on Leigh Hunt.

7 Dines at Lord John Russell's and meets the composer Meyerbeer.

10 Performance of *The Lighthouse* at Campden House, Kensington, in aid of the Bournemouth Sanatorium.

At about the middle of the month, and before the 17th, the Dickens family go to 3 Albion Villas, Folkestone, for their summer holiday (until Oct).

26 Tells Miss Coutts that he is hard at work on his new book.

August

19 (Sun) 'I am in the second number [of *LD* – i.e., chs 5–8]' (to JF).

Towards the end of the month, Anne Brown, who has been with the family for sixteen years, leaves their service in order to marry.

September

16 (Sun) 'I am just now getting to work on number three [chs 9–11]' (to JF).

23 Sends the second number of *LD* to Wills.

30 Tells Wilkie Collins that the third number of *LD* is nearly finished.

October
5   (Fri) Reads *CC* 'in a carpenter's shop, as the biggest place that can be got' at Folkestone (to JF).
11   Presides at a dinner held in honour of Thackeray, who is leaving for a lecture tour in America.
13   Crosses to Boulogne, *en route* for Paris, where Catherine joins him later. In Paris, which becomes the family headquarters until May 1856, they live at 49 avenue des Champs Elysées. During their stay, CD visits London frequently: on 8 November he tells the Hon. Spencer Lyttelton that he comes and goes 'once a month or so'.
24   By this date CD has made an offer for the purchase of Gad's Hill Place (see 7 Feb).

November
During the early part of the month, CD is in London; he is back in Paris by the 10th. There he sits for Ary Scheffer, French portrait-painter, for the portrait now in the National Portrait Gallery.
25   (Sun) Tells Wills that work on *LD* is not going well since he had to put it aside in order to write his Christmas story *The Holly Tree Inn*.

December
1   (Sat) The first number of *LD* appears, continuing monthly to June 1857. 'Memoir of CD', a biographical account, appears in the *Illustrated Times*.
2   'Little Dorrit has beaten even Bleak House out of the field. It is a most tremendous start' (to JF). (The initial printing of 32,000 has been quickly sold out; 6000 further copies of the opening number are called for by the end of the year. See also 6 Jan 1856.)
15   Leaves Paris for London.
17   Goes to Peterborough, where (on the 18th) he gives a reading of *CC* in aid of the Mechanics' Institute.
19   Returns to London.
22   Travels to Sheffield, where he reads *CC* (again in aid of the Mechanics' Institute) to 'enormous effect' (to the Hon. Mrs Watson, 27 Dec). Immediately after the performance, he sets off to return to Paris in order to spend Christmas with his family.

1856

During the early months of the year, the Dickens family continue to reside in Paris.

January
6 (Sun) Tells JF that 'they had sold 35,000 of number two [of *LD*] on new year's day'. (The publicity campaign has included 4000 posters and 310,000 handbills.)

?10 CD is 'just sitting down' to a number of *LD* – presumably the fifth, which he tells Wilkie Collins is 'upon my soul' on the 19th.

19 Sits to the artist Scheffer for four hours. The next day he tells JF that 'The nightmare portrait is nearly done.'

February
CD visits London early in the month.

8 (Fri) Visits Urania Cottage; dines with Lemon and Webster; they go afterwards to the Adelphi Theatre.

9 Visits Gad's Hill Place, which he has agreed to purchase (see 14 Mar), and is 'better pleased with' it 'even than I had prepared myself to be' (to JF, 13 Feb).

11 Returns to Paris.

19 Tells Miss Coutts that he is once again settling down to work on *LD* and is 'in the usual wretchedness of such settlement'.

March
6 (Thurs) Completes the sixth number of *LD*.

9 Travels to London overnight. During his stay in England he learns that JF plans to marry (see 24 Sep).

12 Speaks at the annual meeting of the Royal Literary Fund.

14 Pays the purchase-money (£1750) for Gad's Hill Place.

22 Is back in Paris by this date.

April
18 (Fri) Goes to the theatre to see a French version of *As You Like It*.

21 Dines with the translators engaged on a French version of his works.

29 Leaves Paris and spends a few days at the Royal Ship Hotel, Dover.

May
2 (Fri) Goes to Dover Theatre after walking to Deal and back.

3 Goes to London.
5 Tells his wife that he has not yet begun the eighth number of
   LD.
7 Goes to Drury Lane to see *The Yankee Housekeeper*.
29 Watches the illuminations and fireworks to celebrate the end of
   the Crimean War from the outer gallery of St Paul's.

June
Early in the month, CD goes to Boulogne, where the Dickens family
spend the summer at the Villa des Moulineaux.

July
CD is in London on the 1st but is back in Boulogne by the 5th.
During this month, various friends (Mary Boyle, Wilkie Collins,
Lemon, Stanfield, Webster, Wills) visit Boulogne.
8 (Tues) Tells Macready that *LD* is keeping him busy and that he
   has just begun the tenth number.

August
2 (Sat) Goes to London, but is back in Boulogne within a few
   days.
During the first half of this month, Townshend visits Boulogne. On
account of an epidemic in Paris, the Dickens family cut short their
holiday and return to England; CD follows them about two weeks
later and is once again installed in Tavistock House by 8 September.

September
16 (Tues) Proposes to Wills that Wilkie Collins be taken on the
   regular staff of *HW*.
24 JF marries Mrs Eliza Colburn.

October
4 (Sat) Tells his daughter Mary that preparations for a
   performance of Wilkie Collins's play *The Frozen Deep* have
   begun.
20 A reading of *The Frozen Deep* takes place at Tavistock House.
26 CD goes for a twenty-mile walk, during which he learns his part
   for the play, 'to the great terror of Finchley, Neasden,
   Willesden, and the adjacent country' (to Wilkie Collins).

November

3 (Mon) Rehearsal of *The Frozen Deep*, with which CD is much occupied during this and the next month. Before the rehearsal, CD and Collins dine together to discuss suggestions made by JF, who has read the play in manuscript.

December

15 (Mon) Tells Miss Power that 'The most terrific preparations are in hand' for *The Frozen Deep*.

1857

January

6 (Tues) Performance of *The Frozen Deep*, followed by John Buckstone's farce *Uncle John*, at Tavistock House; CD tells Wills the next day that he is 'perfectly happy with the success'.

8, 12 and 14 Further performances; CD tells Miss Coutts on the 14th that he has 'never seen audiences so affected'.

25 Wilkie Collins dines at Tavistock House.

February

5 (Thurs) CD declines to send his brother Frederick £30 'because I cannot trust you'.

7 CD's forty-fifth birthday; Beard and Wilkie Collins are among the guests at Tavistock House.

13 Visits the Zoological Gardens.

23 Visits Gad's Hill Place.

March

11 (Wed) Speaks at the Annual General Meeting of the Royal Literary Fund.

April

3 (Fri) Invites Hans Andersen to visit Gad's Hill Place in the summer (the two writers had met in July 1847).

During the first half of this month, CD spends about two weeks at Gravesend (Waite's Hotel) with Catherine and Georgina, superintending the renovations at Gad's Hill Place.

6 Speaks at a dinner of the Royal General Theatrical Fund.

May

6 (Wed) Goes to the Borough to see if he can find 'any ruins of the Marshalsea', and finds 'a great part of the original building' (to JF, 7 May). The visit is referred to in the preface to *LD*, dated May 1857.

9 Finishes *LD*.

10 Indian Mutiny begins.

19 A house-warming party is given at Gad's Hill Place; Beard, Wilkie Collins and Wills are among the guests.

21 Takes the chair at a dinner for the Royal Hospital for Incurables.

23 Dines with JF.

24 Dines at a 'solemn Chief Justice's in remote fastnesses beyond Norwood' (to Wilkie Collins, 22 May).

25 Dines with the Geographical Society.

26 Dines at B. W. Procter's.

27 Dines with Wilkie Collins.

30 *LD* is published in volume form.

31 Attends a dinner at Greenwich given by W. H. Russell; his fellow guests include Brooks, Jerrold and Thackeray. Earlier in the day he has walked with Jerrold (see 8 June).

June

1 (Mon) The Dickens family move to Gad's Hill Place for the summer; as usual, CD makes many visits to London during this period.

8 Death of Douglas Jerrold. CD hears the news the next day and at once throws himself into the task of raising money for Jerrold's family.

11 Hans Andersen arrives at Gad's Hill Place for a prolonged visit.

15 With JF, Thackeray, Lemon, Paxton, Milnes and others, CD is a pall-bearer at Jerrold's funeral at Norwood cemetery.

21 Tells JF that he has declined the Queen's invitation to put on a performance of *The Frozen Deep* at the Palace, since he felt uneasy about 'the social position of [his] daughters' in such a situation. The Queen has accepted his suggestion that a private performance be staged for her at the Gallery of Illustration in Regent Street. For the rest of the month, CD is busy with preparations for this performance; rehearsals are held on 26 and 29 June and 2 and 3 July.

30 Gives a charity reading of *CC* at St Martin's Hall, London, in aid of the Douglas Jerrold Fund (see also 24 and 31 July).

July

4   (Sat) *The Frozen Deep* is performed before the Queen (see 21 June), the Prince Consort, the King of Belgium, and an invited audience; it is followed by the farce *Two o'Clock in the Morning*. When the Queen sends for CD after the performance, he begs to be excused from appearing since he is 'in my Farce dress' (to JF, 5 July), and also resists a second invitation.

5   The Queen writes CD a letter 'of the most unofficial and uncourtly character' (to Maclise, 8 July), expressing her pleasure at the performance.

8   Public performance of *The Frozen Deep* in aid of the Douglas Jerrold Fund. There are further performances on the 18th and 25th.

12 CD attends a party given for the members of the cast by Frederick Ouvry at his home, North End Lodge, Walham Green.

15 Andersen's visit comes to an end; CD drives him to Maidstone.

20 Walter Dickens sails for India, having obtained a cadetship in the East India Company's 26th Native Infantry with the help of Miss Coutts. CD travels down to Southampton (on the 19th) for a painful parting.

24 Reads *CC* again at St Martin's Hall in aid of the Douglas Jerrold Fund.

29 Attends a performance of Jerrold's *Black-Eyed Susan* at the Adelphi Theatre.

31 Reads *CC* at Manchester for the Jerrold Fund. Tennyson and his wife are among the audience.

August

20 (Thurs) Travels to Manchester.

21, 22 and 24   Performances of *The Frozen Deep* at the Free Trade Hall, Manchester. Three professional actresses – Ellen Ternan and her mother and sister – join the cast for these performances; CD has previously spent three days (from about the 17th) rehearsing with them in London. After all his efforts for the Jerrold Fund, CD finds himself 'horribly used up' (to Henry Austin, 2 Sep).

September

4   (Fri) CD notes down some 'new ideas for a story' that have

come to him during performances of *The Frozen Deep* (to Miss Coutts, 5 Sep).

5   'What do you think of my paying for this place [Gad's Hill Place], by reviving that old idea of some Readings from my books?' (to JF). Before this time, he appears to have confided in JF concerning his matrimonial problems; in another letter apparently written during this month, he tells him that 'Poor Catherine and I are not made for each other.'

6   'I think I am becoming rather inventive again' (to Wills).

7   CD and Wilkie Collins travel by train to Carlisle to begin a working holiday in the Lake District that results in *The Lazy Tour of Two Idle Apprentices* (written in collaboration and serialised in *HW* from 3 to 31 Oct).

8   They climb Carrick Fell in the dark, and Collins sprains his ankle.

9   At the Ship Hotel, Allonby, Wigton.

11   Back in Carlisle (County Hall).

12   In Lancaster (King's Arms).

15   In Doncaster (Angel Hotel) during race-week. Ellen Ternan is performing in that town.

22   Returns home.

October

11   (Sun) Gives instructions that alterations are to be made to his sleeping-arrangements at Tavistock House. (His dressing-room is converted into his bedroom, and the door communicating with Catherine's – formerly their shared – room is blocked up.)

November

5   (Thurs) Presides at a dinner of the Warehousemen and Clerks' Schools.

December

15   (Wed) Gives a reading of *CC* at Coventry in aid of the Mechanics' Institute.

22   Gives a reading of *CC* at Chatham in aid of the Mechanics' Institute.

1858

January

18 (Mon) CD writes to George Eliot, praising the 'extraordinary merit' of her *Scenes from Clerical Life* (published anonymously in volume form this month), of which she has sent him a copy without disclosing her sex; he also comments to Joseph Landford that if the book, or part of it, were not the work of a woman he would 'begin to believe that I am a woman myself'.

19 Gives a reading of *CC* at Bristol in aid of the Athenaeum.

27 'Growing inclinations of a fitful and undefined sort are upon me sometimes to fall to work on a new book' (to JF).

30 Suggests 'One of these Days' to JF as a possible title for a novel.

February

2 (Tues) Goes to see Westland Marston's *A Hard Struggle* at the Lyceum, 'and cried till I sobbed again' (to JF, 3 Feb).

7 CD's forty-sixth birthday; he dines at Gravesend, Wilkie Collins and JF being the only guests.

9 Presides at a dinner in aid of the Hospital for Sick Children (see also 15 Apr).

March

4 (Thurs) Dines with Wilkie Collins, who reads 'a new play' to him: this is Collins's melodrama *The Red Vial*, with the composition of which CD has given assistance during the winter months, but which is a complete failure when produced in October 1858.

10 Speaks at the Annual General Meeting of the Royal Literary Fund.

16 Tells F. M. Evans that he is considering giving 35–40 readings for money in London and the provinces, with the possibility of later tours in Ireland and America; and asks what influence, if any, this would be likely to have on the reception of his next book. During this month he also discusses the question of the readings with JF, Miss Coutts and Wilkie Collins, and finds JF 'extraordinarily irrational about it' (to Collins, 21 Mar).

21 'The domestic unhappiness remains so strong upon me that I can't write, and (waking) can't rest, one minute. I have never known a moment's peace or content, since the last night of The Frozen Deep [24 Aug 1857]. I do suppose that there never was a

man so seized and rended by one spirit. In this condition though nothing can alter or soften it, I have a turning notion that the mere physical effort and charge of the Readings would be good, as another means of bearing it' (to Wilkie Collins).

26   Gives a reading of *CC* at Edinburgh in aid of the Philosophical Institution.
29   Speaks at a dinner of the Royal General Theatrical Fund.
30   Tells JF that the Queen has expressed a wish to hear his reading of *CC*.

During this month, he tells JF that his marriage is 'all despairingly over. . . . A dismal failure has to be borne, and there an end.'

April
15   (Thurs) Gives a reading at St Martin's Hall in aid of the Hospital for Sick Children.
29   Gives the first of a series of public readings for profit at St Martin's Hall, performing *The Cricket on the Hearth*. The season lasts until 22 July and comprises seventeen readings.

May
1   (Sat) Speaks at the Royal Academy banquet.
6   Reads *The Chimes* at St Martin's Hall.
8   Presides at a dinner of the Artists' Benevolent Fund.
13   Reads *CC* at St Martin's Hall.
14   Thackeray hears rumours of CD's involvement with Ellen Ternan.
20   Reads *Cricket* at St Martin's Hall.
22   Tells Cornelius Felton that Catherine and he have 'agreed to live apart henceforth', the matter having been 'as good as settled' the previous evening 'through Mr Forster's kindness'. (On the 7th, CD has proposed a settlement which JF has apparently communicated to Lemon, who is acting for Catherine; and on the 14th Lemon has written to JF accepting it on her behalf.) At about this time, Catherine moves to 70 Gloucester Crescent, Regent's Park; Charley goes with her, the other children remaining with CD, who makes her an annual allowance of £600.
25   Sends to Arthur Smith a copy of the letter (later known as the 'violated letter') explaining his domestic circumstances.
26   Reads *CC* and (27th) *The Chimes* at St Martin's Hall.
29   At CD's urging, Catherine's mother and sister (Helen) sign a

statement declaring their disbelief in rumours 'deeply affecting the moral character' of CD.

31   Reproves Leech for telling an acquaintance that Charley Dickens 'sides with his mother'.

June

1   (Tues) Presides at a dinner of the Playground and General Recreation Society.
3   Reads *The Chimes*, (9th) *CC*, and (10th) *Dombey* at St Martin's Hall.
12   Publishes in *HW* a statement concerning his 'domestic trouble' and denying 'all the lately whispered rumours'; he has also sent the statement to the newspapers to be copied. Edmund Yates attacks Thackeray in a gossip column in *Town Talk*.
17   Reads at St Martin's Hall (and again on the 23rd and 24th).
26   The committee of the Garrick Club meets to discuss Thackeray's complaint against Yates.

July

1   (Thurs) Reads at St Martin's Hall (and again on the 8th, 14th and 15th).
6   CD speaks in Yates's defence at a general meeting of the Garrick Club.
20   Yates is expelled from the club.
21   CD speaks at a meeting concerning the foundation of a 'Dramatic College' (an institution for retired actors and actresses).
22   Conclusion of CD's London season of readings. CD formally severs relations with F. M. Evans, who has supported Lemon in his refusal to print CD's statement (see 12 June above) in *Punch*. Later he cuts Evans and Lemon when he meets them in the street.

August

1   (Sun) Leaves Gad's Hill Place to begin a provincial reading-tour, accompanied by Arthur Smith, his manager. The tour lasts until 13 November and comprises 83 readings.
2   Reads at Clifton.
3   Reads at Exeter.
4–5   Gives three readings at Plymouth, including a matinée on the 5th.

6   Reads again at Clifton; the audience fight for admission. He is back at Gad's Hill Place for the weekend.

9   Tells Miss Coutts that the first week of the provincial tour was 'an immense success': 'it is a great sensation to have an audience in one's hand'.

10   Resumes readings in Worcester.

11   Reads in Wolverhampton to 'a wonderful audience' (to Mary Dickens, 12 Aug).

12   Reads in Shrewsbury.

13   After reading in Chester, he travels overnight to London and spends the weekend at Gad's Hill Place.

17   In London, where he sees Yates at the *HW* office and then dines with Wills at the Reform Club.

18–21   Gives four readings in Liverpool; the 20th is 'a tremendous night' (to Georgina Hogarth) with an audience of 2300, and the receipts amount to over £200.

21   Takes the night crossing to Dublin, and reads there (23rd–26th) five times.

27   Goes to Belfast and reads there (27th–28th) three times.

30   Goes to Cork via Dublin and reads there.

September

1   (Wed) Reads at Limerick (and again on the 2nd).

3   Leaves Ireland.

4   Is back home with 'a profit of one Thousand Guineas!' (to Wills, 2 Sep) from the Irish readings.

7   In London; visits the *HW* office.

8   Reads in Huddersfield.

9   Reads in Wakefield.

10   Reads in York; on this stage of his provincial tour, CD is accompanied by his two daughters.

11   Reads in Harrogate.

13   Reads twice in Scarborough.

14   Reads in Hull.

15   Reads in Leeds.

16   Reads in Halifax.

17   Reads in Sheffield.

18   Reads in Manchester; then travels overnight to London.

20   During this week he reads in (21st) Darlington, (22nd) Durham, (23rd) Sunderland and (24th and 25th: three performances)

Newcastle, and walks from Durham to Sunderland and from Sunderland to Newcastle.

26   Spends the night at Berwick-upon-Tweed.
27   Goes to Edinburgh for five readings (to 30th inclusive): after a poor house for the first reading, the house is full for the second and for the last two performances hundreds are turned away.

October
1   (Fri) and 2   Reads in Dundee.
4   Reads twice in Aberdeen.
5   Reads in Perth.
6–9   Reads four times in Glasgow.
9   Leaves Glasgow by overnight train, arriving in London on the 10th.
14   Sets off again to read in (14th) Bradford, (15th) Liverpool and (16th) Manchester, but is back in London again for the weekend.
18–20   Gives three readings in Birmingham.
21   Reads in Nottingham.
22   Reads in Derby.
23   Reads in Manchester.
25   Tells Wills that Maria and Ellen Ternan are living at 31 Berners Street, Oxford Street, and that he has sent the eldest Ternan sister (Frances) to Italy, accompanied by her mother, 'to complete a musical education.'
26   Reads in Hull (and again on the 27th).
28   Reads in Leeds.
29   Reads in Sheffield.

November
2   (Tues) Reads in Leamington twice.
3   Reads in Wolverhampton.
4   Reads in Leicester.
5   In London, and at Gad's Hill Place for the weekend.
8   Reads in Reading.
9–10   Gives two readings in Southampton.
11   Gives two readings in Portsmouth.
12–13   In Brighton for three readings. After the afternoon reading on the 13th he dines at the Bedford Hotel with Wilkie Collins.
15   Receives 69 votes in the election for the Lord Rectorship of Glasgow University; Lord Shaftesbury receives 204, and

Bulwer-Lytton is elected with 217. CD has been nominated 'against his express wish' and has made it clear that 'he did not seek election' (Ley).

December

3   (Fri) Presides at a prize-giving at the Institutional Association of Lancashire and Cheshire, held in Manchester.
4   Visits Coventry, where he is presented with a watch at a banquet given in his honour.
22 Takes the chair at a dinner of the Commercial Travellers' Schools.
24 Begins a Christmas season of readings in London; it runs until 8 February and comprises eight readings.
27 Second reading of Christmas season.
29 Gives a charity reading in Chatham.

1859

January

Christmas season continues with readings on 6th, 13th, 20th and 28th.

4   (Tues) CD tells Frith that he is staying at Gad's Hill Place a week longer than planned in order to have 'leisure and quiet to consider something I am turning in my mind'.
24 Asks JF's opinion of *Household Harmony* as a title for his new magazine (the title *All the Year Round* is mentioned four days later).
26 Tells Arthur Smith that he has received an invitation to undertake a reading-tour in America.

During this month CD's portrait is painted by Frith (now in the Forster Collection, Victoria & Albert Museum).

February

Readings on 3rd and 10th.

1   (Tues) Tells Cerjat that he is more popular than he has ever been with the public.

March

11 (Fri) Tells JF that he has chosen the title for *A Tale of Two Cities* and has 'struck out a rather original and bold idea' – i.e. to

publish monthly numbers as well as weekly instalments in *AYR*, a scheme that will 'give me my old standing with my old public'.

April
30 (Sat) The first issue of *AYR* appears, including the first instalment of *TTC*, which runs weekly until 26 November.

May
28 (Sat) *HW* ceases publication; the issue of *AYR* for this date has the words 'with which is incorporated *Household Words*' added to its title. (CD has quarrelled with the *HW* printers, Bradbury and Evans, who are also the publishers of *Punch* [see 22 July 1858], and has refused to continue editing his magazine. On 26 March the Master of the Rolls has ruled that it be sold by auction; and at the auction on 16 May Arthur Smith, acting for CD, has successfully bid for it, whereupon CD has promptly closed it down.)

June
CD spends the summer at Gad's Hill Place, with occasional business trips to London. He suffers a period of ill-health in the early part of the summer.
13 (Mon) Dines with Wilkie Collins and Wills.

July
During this month he is still referring to the possibility of going to America in September, though on the 20th he mentions a postponement (in a letter to J. T. Fields). By 6 August he has definitely decided not to go in 1859, but tells Fields that he may go in a year's time.
9 (Sat) Tells JF that 'The small portions [of *TTC*] drive me frantic'.
10 Tells George Eliot that *Adam Bede* 'has taken its place among the actual experiences and endurances of my life', and invites her to contribute to *AYR* (for their first meeting, see 10 Nov).

August
16 (Tues) Tells Wilkie Collins that 'The Woman in White is the name of names, and very title of titles' (serialisation of Collins's novel begins in *AYR* on 26 Nov). He has been reading

Tennyson's *Idylls of the King* and praises them highly, repeating the praise to JF on the 25th in even more glowing terms.

28   Death of Leigh Hunt (see 24 Dec).

September
Takes a short holiday at Broadstairs (Albion Hotel) in the early part of the month.

October
10   (Mon) At Ipswich, CD begins a short provincial reading-tour lasting until the 27th and comprising fourteen readings.

11–12   In Norwich for two readings.

13   Reads in Bury St Edmunds.

15   Sends the proof-sheets of *TTC* to F. J. Régnier with a view to its being dramatised for the French theatre.

17–18   In Cambridge for two readings.

19   Reads in Peterborough.

20   Reads in Bradford.

21–2   In Nottingham: he reads there on the 21st, but a matinée on the 22nd is cancelled; then to London for the weekend.

24–5   In Oxford for two readings; on the 24th, the audience includes the Prince of Wales (at this time an undergraduate at Christ Church), the Vice-Chancellor, and other notabilities.

26   Reads in Birmingham.

27   Gives two readings in Cheltenham; then proceeds by overnight train to London, thus concluding the second provincial tour.

29   To Gad's Hill Place to celebrate his daughter Kate's birthday.

November
10   (Thurs) Meets George Eliot, who (with Lewes) has invited him to dinner at Holly Lodge, Wandsworth. They have 'a delightful talk about all sorts of things' and discuss 'George Stephenson, the Religion of Humanity etc.' (Lewes's journal).

14   Invites George Eliot to contribute a serial novel to *AYR*, to follow Collins's *Woman in White* (see 14 Feb 1860).

18   Death of Frank Stone. CD goes to Highgate Cemetery the next day 'to choose a Grave' for him (to Wills, 19 Nov).

26   Serialisation of *TTC* is concluded.

December
20   (Tues) Invites Mrs Gaskell to contribute a serial novel to *AYR*.

22   Presides at a dinner for the Commercial Travellers' School.
24   Publishes 'Leigh Hunt: A Remonstrance' in *AYR*. Begins a short Christmas season of three London readings with a matinée at St Martin's Hall; other readings there on 26 December and 2 January (his last appearances in that building, which burned down in Aug 1860).

1860

January
2   (Mon) CD concludes his Christmas season of London readings.
7   Writes to Wilkie Collins in praise of *The Woman in White*, of which he has read a portion in manuscript.
9   Attends the funeral of Lord Macaulay (died 28 Dec).
During this month the series of essays *The Uncommercial Traveller* begins publication in *AYR*.

February
14   (Tues) Calls on Lewes to discuss George Eliot's withdrawal from her agreement to contribute a novel to *AYR*.
21   Tells Charles Lever that, on account of George Eliot's withdrawal, he wishes to begin serialisation of Lever's *A Day's Ride* in July.

March
8   (Thurs) Presides at a dinner of the Royal Society of Musicians.

April
17   (Tues) Presides at a lecture given by Layard at the Mechanics' Institute, Chatham. During his visit to Kent, Layard is a guest at Gad's Hill Place.

July
17   (Tues) Marriage of Kate Dickens and Charles Collins at Higham, Kent. Among the guests are Beard, Mary Boyle, Chorley, Fechter, Fitzgerald, Holman Hunt, Kent, Townshend and Wills; the bride's mother is not present.
27   CD is summoned to Manchester on account of his brother Alfred's illness; by the time he arrives, Alfred is dead, leaving a

widow and five children – 'you may suppose to whom' (to Mrs Dickinson, 19 Aug).

28   Returns to Gad's Hill Place, accompanied by Alfred's widow.

29   Congratulates Wilkie Collins on the completion of *The Woman in White* ('your best book').

31   Dines with Wilkie Collins.

August

1   (Wed) Attends Alfred's funeral at Highgate Cemetery.

3   Invites Bulwer-Lytton to write a novel for *AYR*.

21   Completes the sale of Tavistock House to J. P. Davis, who takes possession on 4 September.

September

3   (Mon) Burns, 'in the field at Gad's Hill, the accumulated letters and papers of twenty years' (to Wills, 4 Sep).

14   Tells the Hon. Mrs Watson that he is 'on the restless eve of beginning a new big book'.

24   Goes to Portsmouth with his son Sydney, who has passed his examination as a naval cadet and is now joining his training-ship. By this time the Dickens children are widely scattered: Charley, who – after Eton and a period in Germany – has been employed for three or four years by Barings, a London import firm, has recently gone to the Far East to learn the import trade (he returns to England in Jan 1861, and is reported to Cerjat on 16 Mar 1862 as 'in business as an Eastern merchant in the City [of London]'); Walter is in the army in India (see 31 Dec 1863); Kate (see 17 July above) is on a prolonged honeymoon in France; Frank, who has studied in France and Germany, still lives at home but is in business in London with a view to joining Charley when the latter sets up his own business (though in the event Frank soon joins the staff of *AYR* and, proving of little use there, goes to India (see Jan 1864) and later to Canada and the USA); Alfred is at school in France; Mary lives at home and keeps house for her father (but is currently on a month's holiday in Scotland); Henry is at school; Edward is being taught at home by a private tutor, but is shortly afterwards sent to school.

Near the end of the month, work begins on *Great Expectations*.

October

2 (Tues) CD holds a 'council of war' at the *AYR* office; it is decided that the serialisation of *GE* will begin on 1 December, in an attempt to reverse the recent decline in readership (see next entry).

6 Tells Lever that serialisation of *GE* will proceed alongside that of Lever's *A Day's Ride*, which has failed to seize the interest of readers. Charles Reade, whom CD has invited to contribute a novel to *AYR*, dines with CD.

24 Tells Wilkie Collins that he has completed four instalments of *GE* – i.e. the first seven chapters of the novel.

November

1 (Thurs) Goes to Bideford, North Devon, with Wilkie Collins.

2–4 They tour Cornwall, arriving in Liskeard on the afternoon of the 3rd, and spending the 4th in the neighbourhood of that town.

5 Returns to London. The Christmas story *A Message from the Sea*, written jointly with Collins and set in Clovelly, uses material gathered during the Cornish tour.

During this month, work on *GE* is interrupted by work on the Christmas story.

December

1 (Sat) Serialisation of *GE* begins in *AYR*, continuing weekly until 3 August 1861.

18 Gives a charity reading at the Mechanics' Institute, Chatham. (The Institute is referred to in 'Dullborough Town', included in *UT*.)

21 Attends a pantomime at Covent Garden.

28 Tells Mary Boyle that he is 'not quite well' and is 'being doctored'; he is staying at the *AYR* office (11 Wellington Street), working at *GE* and visiting the theatre every night. His physician is Dr Frank Beard, and an 'old servant' looks after him at the *AYR* apartment.

1861

January

1 (Tues) CD goes with Wilkie Collins to see 'Buckley's Serenaders', a variety show at the St James's Hall.

9   Tells Georgina Hogarth that he is 'gradually getting well'. By this date, CD and Collins have decided to sue a Mr Lane of the Britannia Theatre, who has announced an unauthorised dramatisation of *A Message from the Sea*.

12   Publishes in *The Times* a letter on dramatic rights in works of fiction.

25   Tells Mrs Cowden Clarke that *GE* is 'an immense success'.

By the end of the month, he has, for the sake of his unmarried daughter Mary, rented a furnished house in London (3 Hanover Terrace, Regent's Park) until June.

March

14   (Thurs) Begins a season of six readings at the St James's Hall, continuing to 18 April. (Other readings on 22 and 28 Mar, 4, 11 and 18 Apr.)

April

1   (Mon) Speaks at a Mansion House banquet.

18   Conclusion of spring season of London readings.

May

?23 (Thurs) Goes to Dover for a short holiday (Lord Warden Hotel).

24   Walks to Folkestone and back. Tells Wilkie Collins that he hopes to finish *GE* by about 12 June.

June

7   (Fri) Tells Bulwer-Lytton that he has been writing 'hard all day'. He is back in London by this date.

11   Tells Macready that he has just finished *GE* and is 'the worse for wear'.

15   Accompanied by Georgina and Mary, CD visits Bulwer-Lytton at Knebworth for a long weekend. Bulwer-Lytton returns the visit in July.

19   Dines at the Mansion House.

July

1   (Mon) Tells JF that, at Bulwer-Lytton's urging, he has written a new ending for *GE*.

11   Leech and his wife spend a long weekend at Gad's Hill Place.

August

3   (Sat) Serialisation of *GE* in *AYR* is concluded.

28 Tells Wilkie Collins that he has 'got the Copperfield reading ready for delivery' and is going to 'blaze away at Nickleby' – i.e. he is preparing for the next reading-tour.

31 Spends the day at Sheerness; his guests include Mary Boyle and Marcus Stone. Tells Wills that he works 'every day for two or three hours on my Readings'.

September

9   (Mon) Recommends Miss Maria Ternan to Benjamin Webster, theatrical manager, telling him that he has 'a high opinion of the young lady and take[s] a strong interest in her and her family'.

15 Layard is on a visit to Gad's Hill Place.

October

1   (Tuesday) Death of Arthur Smith, manager of the reading-tours: CD later tells JF that 'it is as if my right arm were gone', and tells Macready that Smith's death has caused him 'great distress and anxiety'.

8   Visits Henry Austin at Ealing.

9   Austin having died during the night, CD visits Ealing again to take charge of the funeral arrangements.

14 Attends Austin's funeral (he has attended Smith's earlier in the month).

28 Season of 46 provincial readings begins at Norwich ('a very lumpish audience indeed': to Georgina Hogarth, 29 Oct), and Smith is sorely missed. (His successor, Thomas Headland, is proving unsatisfactory.)

29 Another reading in Norwich.

30 In Bury St Edmunds.

31 In Ipswich.

November

1   (Fri) In Colchester.

3   At Gad's Hill Place.

4   Reads at Canterbury, then (5th) at Dover and (6th) at Hastings.

7–9 Gives three readings at Brighton.

21–3 In Newcastle for three readings. On the 22nd, CD's aplomb calms the audience and averts a panic and possible tragedy after his 'gas-apparatus' suddenly falls down during a performance.

24–5   In Berwick-upon-Tweed, where he reads on the 25th.
26   Goes to Edinburgh, where he remains until 2 December and enjoys 'Blazes of triumph' (to Wills, 1 Dec), giving five readings (27th, 28th, two on the 30th, and 2 Dec).

December
3   (Tues) In Glasgow for four readings (to the 6th).
9–10   In Carlisle for two readings.
11–12   In Lancaster for a reading on the 12th.
13   Reads in Preston.
14   Reads in Manchester.
15   In Liverpool; but cancels his readings there and in Chester on account of the Prince Consort's death on the previous day, and returns to London, spending Christmas Day at Gad's Hill Place.
30–31   Resumes the reading-tour with two readings at Birmingham.

1862

January
1   (Wed) In Leamington for two readings.
2   Travels from Leamington to Cheltenham, where he dines with Macready, who now resides there.
3–4   Reads in Cheltenham.
5   At Gad's Hill Place; then to Plymouth for two readings (6th and 7th).
8–9   In Torquay. CD reads on the 8th and on the afternoon of the 9th; an evening reading on the 9th is cancelled on account of his illness (probably exhaustion).
10–11   Gives two readings in Exeter.
11   Returns to London.
16   Gives a charity reading at the Mechanics' Institute, Chatham.
23   Dines at the *AYR* office with Wilkie Collins and Wills; after dinner they go to a pantomime.
25   Resumes the reading-tour with a reading at Manchester.
27–30   In Liverpool for three readings postponed in the previous month.
30   Reads at Chester, concluding the present tour, and then travels overnight to London.

February

1 (Sat) At Gad's Hill Place.
7 CD's fiftieth birthday. Dines with JF and Wilkie Collins.
25 By this date he has moved into 16 Hyde Park Gate, having exchanged houses with a friend for the next three months. (On 5 Apr he describes it to Beard as 'the nastiest little house in London'.)

March

1 (Sat) Attends the first of H. F. Chorley's series of lectures on 'National Music'.
13 Begins a series of eleven readings at the St James's Hall, continuing to 27 June. (Other readings on 20 and 27 Mar, 3, 10 and 24 Apr, 7, 17 and 21 May, 6 and 19 June.)
29 Presides at a dinner of the Artists' General Benevolent Institution.

May

20 (Tues) Presides at a dinner of the Newsvendors' Benevolent Institution.

June

19 (Thurs) Conclusion of the series of London readings.
28 Tells JF that he has been offered £10,000 to visit Australia. He takes the offer seriously, referring to it again in a letter to JF on 22 October, and to Beard, whom he sounds on the question of accompanying him, on 4 November. Bulwer-Lytton urges him to go; but Beard declines his invitation and CD tells him on 24 December that he probably will not go.
During this month he goes to France on holiday; he returns to England to finish off the series of readings, but resumes his holiday early in July. (Ellen Ternan very probably accompanies him.)

July

27 (Sun) Georgina Hogarth, who has been unwell for some time, is now 'very, very poorly' (to Wilkie Collins). Her illness continues throughout the summer; by 20 September she is 'better', though still 'very weak' (to Collins).

August

4 (Mon) to 6 CD is at Dover and visits Wilkie Collins at

Broadstairs. On the 6th, JF and his wife visit Gad's Hill Place.
25   'I am trying to coerce my thought into hammering out the
     Christmas number [*Somebody's Luggage*]' (to JF).

September
19   (Fri) Leech dines with CD, and they afterwards go with
     Georgina to see a very bad play at the Adelphi Theatre.

October
 4   (Sat) to 6   Macready spends the weekend at Gad's Hill Place.
16   CD leaves for the Continent.
17   In Hazebrouck; visits Dunkirk.
19   Meets Georgina and Mary at Boulogne, they having just made
     the crossing, and escorts them to Paris.

November
15   (Sat) Wills visits CD in Paris for a few days.
17   CD sends condolences to Mrs Maria Winter on her father's
     death.
28   Returns to London for a weekend on business, and dines with
     Yates. Then returns to Paris.

December
10   (Wed) Visits England briefly on account of his friend Elliotson,
     whose health is giving serious concern.
22   Leaves Paris with Georgina and Mary to spend the Christmas
     season at Gad's Hill Place.

1863

January
 8   (Thurs) to 11   During this period, as at many other times, CD is
     at the *AYR* office. After the 11th (he has told Wilkie Collins on
     the 1st) he will 'vanish into space for a day or two', the
     vanishing no doubt being in the direction of Ellen Ternan.
15   Returns to Paris.
17   Gives the first of three triumphantly successful readings (others
     on the 29th and 30th) for charity at the British Embassy, Paris.
31   Goes to the Opéra with Lady Molesworth to see Gounod's
     Faust.

February

5   (Thurs) Leaves Paris for a short tour.
7   CD's fifty-first birthday; he is in Arras.
19 Back in London by this date.

March

2   (Mon) Begins a series of thirteen readings at the Hanover Square Rooms, lasting until 12 June. (Others on 11 and 13 March, 21, 23 and 28 Apr, 5, 8, 15, 22 and 29 May, 5 and 12 June.) Thereafter CD gives no further paid readings until 1866.
15 Beard visits Gad's Hill Place.
16 With Georgina and Mary, CD attends a birthday-party at Charles Knight's.
26 Death of Augustus Egg in Algiers.

April

4   (Sat) At short notice, CD replaces Wilkie Collins and presides at a dinner of the Royal General Theatrical Fund.

May

6   (Wed) Presides at a dinner for the Royal Free Hospital.

June

12 (Fri) Concludes series of London readings.

July

From this month, Henry and Edward Dickens produce during their school holidays the *Gad's Hill Gazette*, a family newspaper, of which over thirty issues appear irregularly until the beginning of 1866, and to which CD is an occasional contributor.

August

5   (Wed) Death of Mrs Georgina Hogarth, mother-in-law of CD.

September

13 (Sun) Death of Elizabeth Dickens, mother of CD.
14 Tells Wills that work has begun on the new Christmas story, to be titled *Mrs Lirriper's Lodgings*.

October

8   (Thurs) *The Times* publishes a letter from CD on the earthquake

shock that occurred on the 6th. CD tells JF that he is 'exceedingly anxious to begin my book [*Our Mutual Friend*] – I see my opening perfectly, with the one main line on which the story is to turn'. He tells JF that he intends to have five numbers in hand before publication begins. (The title had been settled on, and some of the main lines of the plot sketched out, as early as 1861; in Apr 1862 he had confessed that he had tried repeatedly and in vain to make a start; in Aug 1863 he was 'full of notions' for the new novel.) (See also 25 Jan 1864.)

November
During this month, work continues on *Mrs Lirriper's Lodgings* and on the early chapters of *OMF*.

December
15 (Tues) Gives a charity reading at Chatham.
24 Death of W. M. Thackeray. CD attends the funeral at Kensal Green Cemetery on the 30th, and publishes a tribute in the *Cornhill Magazine* in February 1864. (CD and Thackeray had quarrelled and become estranged in 1858, but a reconciliation has taken place some months before Thackeray's death, probably in early May.)
31 New Year's Eve party at Gad's Hill Place; CD plays at charades with his children. His son Walter dies in Calcutta on this day, but news does not reach CD until early in February.

1864

January
25 (Mon) CD tells Wilkie Collins that *Mrs Lirriper's Lodgings* has been a greater success than any of his previous Christmas stories, with about 220,000 copies sold; also that the first two numbers of *OMF* are finished and he is just beginning the third number.
At the end of the month, Frank Dickens leaves for India to join his brother Walter (not knowing, of course, that the latter has died on 31 Dec).

February
Early in the month, CD rents 57 Gloucester Place, Hyde Park, for a

few months, 'to be in town when my book is preparing and begins to come out' (to Miss Coutts, 12 Feb, by which date he is installed there).

23 (Tues) Advises Marcus Stone on the illustrations for *OMF*.
25 Tells JF that he has been with Stone to see a shop in St Giles's that becomes the model for Mr Venus's establishment in *OMF*.

March
29 (Tues) Tells JF that he is writing 'very slowly'.

April
6 (Wed) Presides at a dinner for the Printers' Pension Society.
12 Presides at a dinner for University College Hospital.
23 Celebrates Shakespeare's birthday with Browning and Wilkie Collins.
30 Publication of the first number of *OMF*, which continues monthly to November 1865.

May
3 (Tues) *OMF* is selling well – 'now in his thirtieth thousand, and orders flowing in fast' (to JF). However, the initial printing of 40,000 was over-optimistic, and the print order for the second number is reduced to 35,000.
9 Dines with Fechter.
11 Presides at a meeting for the establishment of the Shakespeare Foundation Schools.

June
1 (Wed) Dines with Bulwer-Lytton.
10 Is about to begin the seventh number of *OMF*.
Towards the end of the month, CD leaves for a short continental holiday (approximately 26 June to 7 July), presumably in the company of Ellen Ternan. A letter of 26 June to Mrs Mary Nichols states that his destination is Belgium; but on the same date he implies to Wills that he is going to Paris, and refers to his excursion as a 'Mysterious Disappearance'.

July
29 (Fri) Tells JF that he has been 'wanting in invention' and has 'fallen back' with *OMF*: 'This week I have been very unwell; am still out of sorts; and as I know from two days' slow experience,

have a very mountain to climb before I shall see the open country of my work'; also that 'Looming large before me is the Christmas work [*Mrs Lirriper's Legacy*].'

August
Towards the end of the month, the Forsters spend a long weekend at Gad's Hill Place.

October
1 (Sat) Tells Wills that he has finished the ninth number of *OMF* and has begun *Mrs Lirriper's Legacy*.
8 Tells Wills that he hopes to finish the Christmas story within two or three days, and describes himself as 'something the worse for work'.
In the middle of the month, CD goes to Dover (Lord Warden Hotel) for a few days' rest.
29 Death of Leech. In November CD tells JF that the loss has put him out 'woefully' and that he has been unable to work for two days.

December
Christmas guests at Gad's Hill Place include JF and Fechter and their wives, also Stone and Chorley.

1865

January
7 (Sat) CD tells JF that construction of the Swiss chalet sent (in 58 boxes) as a gift from the actor Charles Fechter is proceeding 'excellently': it is being erected in the garden at Gad's Hill Place, and CD often works there in his last years.

February
15 (Wed) Tells Mrs Procter, 'when I am, as I am now, very hard at work upon a book [*OMF*], I never will dine out more than one day in a week'.
25 Resigns from the Garrick Club (as Wilkie Collins also does), after Wills, whom they have proposed for membership, has been blackballed.
In the latter part of the month, CD suffers from a frost-bitten foot as

the result of taking a long walk in deep snow. The foot is still causing him pain and sleeplessness in the latter part of March; by 22 April he is able to 'walk my ten miles in the morning without inconvenience' once again, but is 'absurdly obliged to sit shoeless all the evening' (to Macready).

March
During this month, CD rents 16 Somers Place, Hyde Park, until June.

April
22 (Sat) CD reports himself to Macready as 'working like a dragon' at *OMF*.
27 Goes out to dinner for the first time since suffering from frost-bite (see 25 Feb).

May
9 (Tues) Presides at a dinner of the Newsvendors' Benevolent Institution.
17 Writes to Layard, soliciting letters of introduction for his son Alfred, who is going to Australia 'to make his way in the new world'.
20 Presides at a dinner of the Newspaper Press Fund.
29 Alfred Dickens sails for Melbourne.
During this month, CD tells JF, 'If I were not going away now, I should break down.' The reference is to a visit to France with Ellen Ternan, presumably beginning at the end of May or in very early June.

June
9 (Fri) On the way back from France, while travelling between Dover and London, CD and Ellen are involved in the Staplehurst railway accident, in which ten are killed and about fifty injured. Although the carriage in which they are travelling goes off the rails and hangs suspended over the sides of the collapsed bridge, CD is 'not touched, scarcely shaken' (to Frank Beard, 10 June). Having climbed out of the carriage, and presumably rescued Ellen (and possibly her mother, who may have been travelling with them), he goes back in order to retrieve the manuscript of a portion of *OMF* (see the Postscript to that novel); then he works 'for hours among the dying and dead' (to JF, 10 June).

11   Writes to Catherine, presumably to reassure her of his safety.
14   Is 'too shaken to write many notes' (to Louis B. Winter).

July
 1   (Sat) Turk, CD's mastiff, is killed by a train; another pet, Linda (a
     Saint Bernard), escapes with a minor injury.
29   CD attends the opening of the Guild Houses at Knebworth, in
     the company of JF, Kent, Knight, Reade, Wills, Yates and
     others; they visit a new public house named Our Mutual
     Friend, and go on to a gathering at Knebworth Hall, where CD
     delivers a speech.

August
 7   (Mon) Chorley and Fechter arrive for a stay at Gad's Hill Place.
     CD attends the annual treat for Sunday School pupils held in
     the meadow adjoining the house.
19   The *Gad's Hill Gazette* records that CD has been suffering from
     neuralgia for the past week.
23   Sends a portion of the manuscript of the final double number of
     OMF to the printers.
27   Tells Wills that he is working 'like a Dragon' and hopes to finish
     OMF in about a week.

September
 2   (Sat) Finishes *OMF*. He then goes off for a short holiday in
     Paris, returning on the 14th.
Later in the month he writes a preface for a new edition of Adelaide
Anne Procter's *Legends and Lyrics* (finished by the 26th), and also
begins work on his Christmas story *Dr Marigold's Prescriptions*.
28   Attends a meeting of the Guild of Literature and Art.

November
 6   (Mon) Tells Kent that he has been 'unwell with a relaxed
     throat'. By this date he has shown the manuscript of his new
     Christmas story to JF.
 7   Dines with Chorley.

December
18   (Mon) Layard dines at Gad's Hill Place.
19   CD gives a charity reading at Chatham.
     Christmas guests at Gad's Hill Place include, among others,
     Chorley, Charles and Kate Collins, Fechter and Stone.

31 At the New Year's Eve celebrations at Gad's Hill Place, Buzz, Crambo, Spanish Merchant and other games are played: 'As the clock struck twelve, the usual formula was gone through, and Mr John Thompson favoured the company with the chimes of the gong' (*Gad's Hill Gazette*).

1866

January

6 (Sat) CD tells Mary Boyle that he cannot make up his mind whether to give another series of London readings, but that if he decides to do so it will probably be 'on a large scale' (see 23 March).

9 Receives a copy of Bulwer-Lytton's *The Lost Tales of Miletus*, reads it at once (finishing it after midnight), and rereads it the next day. On the 18th he describes it to Kent as 'a most noble book'.

10 Dines with Captain and Mrs Stewart at Chatham Dockyard; among the other guests is Captain Randolph, formerly of the *Orlando*, on which Sydney Dickens has served as a midshipman.

16 Proposes the Mayoress's health at a Mansion House banquet.

19 Drives through deep snow to dine with Lord and Lady Darnley at Cobham.

25 W. H. Russell visits Gad's Hill Place.

26 CD gives a dinner party for eighteen, followed by dancing.

31 Gives a reading at Myddleton Hall, Islington – the first paid reading for about two and a half years.

February

During this month, CD rents 6 Southwick Place, Hyde Park, until June.

8 (Thurs) CD's doctor, Frank Beard, gives him a thorough examination; the next day CD tells Georgina that Beard has diagnosed 'degeneration of some functions of the heart. It does not contract as it should', and has prescribed iron, quinine and digitalis. CD adds that for some time he has been aware of 'a decided change in my buoyancy and hopefulness'. Shortly afterwards, he secures a second opinion from a Dr Brinton of Brook Street. Within a few weeks he tells JF that 'tonics have

already brought me round', and that he has accepted an offer to give thirty readings for £50 a night, all expenses paid. (After the examination by Beard on the 8th, he dines with Beard and Wilkie Collins.)

14 Presides at a dinner of the Dramatic, Equestrian and Musical Sick Fund Association.

March

11 (Sun) Tells JF that plans for the reading-tour are going ahead, and that he has prepared a new reading, *Doctor Marigold*, 'with immense pains'.

23–4 Gives two readings at Cheltenham, where CD stays with Macready.

28 Speaks at a dinner of the Royal General Theatrical Fund.

April

10 (Tues) Begins season of thirty readings in London and the provinces for Chappell (see 8 Feb and 2 Aug) with a reading of *Doctor Marigold* at the St James's Hall. Dolby is now his manager.

11 Accompanied by Dolby and Wills, as well as a servant and a gasman, CD travels to Liverpool (Adelphi Hotel) and reads in the St George's Hall in the evening.

12 Reads in the Free Trade Hall, Manchester, and returns to Liverpool the same evening.

13 Second reading in Liverpool; 3000 people are turned away. CD later reports himself to Georgina as 'tired'; he is still taking his 'tonic' (see 8 Feb). The next day he tells Mary Dickens that he cannot sleep.

14 Gives a third reading (a matinée) in Liverpool; in the evening he goes to a circus with Dolby.

16 Travels to Glasgow, and reads there the next day.

18 In Edinburgh for a reading.

19 Travels to Glasgow with Wills (Dolby has gone ahead), and reads there in the evening.

20–1 Two more readings in Edinburgh (the second a matinée).

24 Back in London for a reading there.

25 Travels north again and gives (26th) a reading in Manchester and (27th–28th) two more in Liverpool.

May

1 (Tues) Reads at St James's Hall, London.

2 Reads at the Crystal Palace. Writing from Gad's Hill Place, CD tells J. T. Fields, 'I really do not know that any sum of money that could be laid down would induce me to cross the Atlantic to read' (see also 2 Aug 1866, 10 and 20 May, 6 and 13 June, 3 Aug 1867, etc.).

4 Reads at Greenwich.

7 Presides at a dinner of the Metropolitan Rowing Clubs.

9 Reads in Clifton.

10 Reads in Birmingham.

11 Reads in Clifton again; is suffering from a cold and is 'not at all well' (to Georgina Hogarth).

14 Reads in London.

15 Sets off for Aberdeen, and reads there on the 16th.

17 Travels from Aberdeen to Glasgow, breaking the journey at Perth; reports himself to JF as 'in a condition the reverse of flourishing; half strangled with my cold, and dyspeptically gloomy and dull'; but 'a lovely walk' at Perth makes him feel better.

18 In Glasgow for a reading.

19 Reads in Edinburgh.

22 Reads in London.

24–5 Gives two readings in Portsmouth. During his stay in that city, CD revisits Southsea; and in the course of a walk with Dolby, 'turning the corner of a street suddenly', they find themselves in Landport Terrace. 'The name of the street catching Mr Dickens' eye, he suddenly exclaimed, "By Jove! here is the place where I was born"'; and, acting on his suggestion, we walked up and down the terrace for some time, speculating as to which of the houses had the right to call itself his cradle' (CD apparently did not succeed in identifying the house) (Dolby, *CD as I Knew Him*, pp. 37–8).

28 At Gad's Hill Place.

29 Reads in London.

June

5 (Tues) Reads in London.

8 Tells Macready that the success of the present series of readings has been 'quite astounding'.

12 The season of readings concludes with a final reading in London.

29 JF visits Gad's Hill Place.

August

2 (Mon) Tells S. Arthur Chappell of the firm of Chappell, concert agents, for whom the recently concluded series of readings has been undertaken, that he is prepared to undertake another series in the new year, and suggests forty readings at £60 each, all expenses paid, or (in round figures) 42 readings for £2500; the latter offer is accepted. He tells Dolby that he has received 'a very large proposal from America, but cannot bear the thought of the distance and absence'. On this day he writes from Eton, allegedly while waiting for a train 'after a walk'; the next day he writes to another correspondent from Windsor, this time describing himself as 'merely walking in the Park'. Ellen Ternan is perhaps installed in a house in Slough, not far from Eton and Windsor, by this date.

7 Tells Wills that his next Christmas story 'continues to reside in the Limbo of the Unborn'.

During this month, CD tells JF that, once the Christmas story and the next series of readings are over, he hopes to get down to 'a new story for our prepared new series of All the Year Round early in the spring [of 1867]' (this notion did not materialise).

September

6 (Thurs) Asks Dr Beard for a prescription for a 'disagreeable pain in the pit of the stomach and chest'. During this month, he tells JF that twice in one week he has been 'seized in a most distressing manner – apparently in the heart; but, I am persuaded, only in the nervous system'.

October

4 (Thurs) Describes himself to Wilkie Collins as 'in Christmas Labour' – i.e. at work on his Christmas story, *Mugby Junction*.

23 Attends a rehearsal of a dramatic version of Wilkie Collins's novel *Armadale*.

December

14 (Wed) Tells William Kent that *Mugby Junction* has sold 211,000 copies; by Christmas Day it has passed a quarter-million.

26 Organises 'footraces and rustic sports . . . for the villagers' in a field at Gad's Hill Place (to Macready, 28 Dec; to JF, 25 Dec). Some 2000 people attend.

27 Kate, who has been ill, arrives at Gad's Hill Place with her husband.

1867

January

1 (Tues) CD is at work on two new items based on *Mugby Junction* and devised for his impending reading-tour.

15 Begins a new series of readings with a performance at the St James's Hall. This series, the second organised by Chappell, lasts until 13 May and comprises 52 readings in London and the provinces.

16 Travels to Liverpool, accompanied by his manager Dolby and his valet Scott, and (18th–19th) gives two readings there.

22 To Chester by Mersey ferry 'in a blinding snow-storm and a furious easterly gale' (Dolby). He reads in Chester in a hall 'like a Methodist chapel, in low spirits, and with a cold in its head' (to Mary Dickens).

23 Reads in Wolverhampton; immediately after the reading, he travels to Birmingham in a state of exhaustion.

24 Reads in Birmingham.

25 Reads in Leicester.

29 Reads in London; afterwards he is 'very tired' but 'cannot sleep' (to JF).

31 Reads in Leeds.

During this month, *George Silverman's Explanation* begins serialisation in the *Atlantic Monthly*, continuing until March.

February

1 (Fri) Second reading in Leeds.

2 Reads in Manchester.

3 Returns to London, 'so shaken with railways that I can hardly write' (to Mrs Frances Elliot, 4 Feb). On the 12th, he tells Wilkie Collins that since the Staplehurst accident (see 9 June 1865) he 'feel[s] them [railways] very much'.

8–9 Two readings in Bath; he returns to London after the second.

12   Reads in London.
13   Reads in Birmingham.
14–15   Gives two readings in Liverpool; spends the morning of the 15th walking on the sands at New Brighton.
16   Reads in Manchester; then sets off for Glasgow at 1.45 a.m.
18   Reads in Glasgow; while there he loses 'a considerable quantity of blood' (to Dr Beard, to whom he explains that he is suffering from piles).
20   In Bridge of Allan for a rest; with Dolby, he walks to Stirling (three miles), where they visit the jail, and back again.
21   Back in Glasgow for another reading.
22–3   In Edinburgh for two readings; the final reading of the Scottish tour is given on the afternoon of the 23rd; then travels overnight to London.
26   Reads in London.
27   At Gad's Hill Place.
28   Reads at York.

March
1   (Fri) Reads in Bradford. He thanks Mrs Eliza Davis for the gift of a Hebrew and English Bible. (On 10 July 1863 he had defended himself against her charge that the character of Fagin in *OT* did an injustice to the Jewish people; had stated that he entertained 'friendly' feelings towards them; and had sent her a donation for a Jewish charity. In a later letter [16 Nov 1864] he had told her how he hoped to be 'the best of friends with the Jewish people'.)
4–5   Gives two readings in Newcastle.
5   Tells a correspondent that during his reading-tours he is followed by a 'pursuing shower' of proofs for *AYR*.
6   Reads in Leeds.
7   Reads in Wakefield, then returns to Gad's Hill Place.
12   Reads in London.
13   Sets off for Ireland, travelling overnight to Holyhead through a snowstorm; in Wales, the engine has to be dug out of the snow blocking the line.
14   Arrives in Holyhead in the early morning; embarks at 2 p.m. for the four-hour crossing to Dublin, where he stays until the 19th giving readings on the 15th and 18th.
19   Travels to Belfast, and reads there on the 20th. On the latter date he tells Mrs Frances Elliot that he has had a 'tremendous

success' in Ireland, 'notwithstanding the Fenian alarms' (earlier in the month there had been Fenian uprisings near Dublin and elsewhere).

21   Returns to Dublin, and reads again there on the 22nd.
23   Returns to London; then proceeds to Slough, where he remains until the 25th.
26   Reads in London.
28   Reads in Cambridge – 'the success the most brilliant I have ever seen' (to Georgina, 29 Mar).
29   Reads in Norwich.

April
3   (Wed) Travels to Gloucester and reads there.
4   Reads in Swansea.
5–6   Gives two readings in Cheltenham, returning after the second (a matinée) to Gad's Hill Place for the weekend.
8   Reads in London. As Dolby notes (*CD as I Knew Him*, p. 82), 'Nearly every week we were in London for a Reading in St James's Hall, and on the following morning we were on our way to some provincial town'. Dolby also notes that during the visits to London CD was dealing with a heavy correspondence and with the editorial work for *AYR*.
10   Reads in Worcester.
11   Reads in Hereford.
12   Reads in Clifton.
13   In Slough, where Ellen Ternan is living.
14–21   During Holy Week, takes a holiday from the reading-tour. He is at Gravesend with Georgina on the 15th; at Gad's Hill Place 16th–17th; goes to Slough with Wills on the 19th; returns to London on the 20th; and is back at Gad's Hill Place on the 21st.
23   To Slough again.
24   Travels to Preston for a reading on the 25th; he and Dolby walk thence to Blackburn, where he reads on the 26th.
27   Goes to Slough for the weekend.
29   Reads in London.
30   Reads in Stoke-on-Trent.

May
1   (Wed) Reads in Hanley. CD suggests to Wilkie Collins that they should collaborate on the next Christmas story.

2 Reads in Warrington; then back to Gad's Hill Place for the weekend.

8 Reads in Croydon.

9 Dines at the Athenaeum; then goes to the Lyceum Theatre, where Ellen is also present.

10 Goes to Slough. Tells a correspondent that he begins to feel himself 'drawn towards America' on account of the 'enormous' expenses in which he is involved.

13 Reads at the St James's Hall, thus concluding the series.

14 Tells JF that he has worked very hard at perfecting his readings, and has committed them all to memory.

18 Death of Stanfield. CD had visited him shortly before the end. CD's obituary appears in *AYR* on 1 June.

20 'If I ever go [to America], the time would be when the Christmas number goes to press. Early in this next November. . .' (to JF).

21 Dines with Beard and Wilkie Collins.

27 Attends Stanfield's funeral; at the graveside he meets Lemon and they are reconciled and embrace 'affectionately' (to Lemon's son, 25 May 1870). (For their estrangement, see 22 July 1858.)

June

2 (Sun) At Gad's Hill Place, 'alone with G[eorgina]' (diary).

5 Presides at a dinner of the Railway Benevolent Society.

6 Gives Wills his reasons for going to America, among which are the large profits to be made (he estimates £10,000) and the favourable effect on the sales of the Charles Dickens Edition. Dines with JF to discuss whether he should go.

13 Tells J. T. Fields, in strict confidence, that Dolby will go to America in August to investigate the feasibility of a tour.

21 Dines at the Athenaeum; then goes to Peckham for the weekend (to the 24th) – Ellen now presumably being installed there.

30 Reads the first three instalments of Collins's *The Moonstone* (intended for *AYR*) in manuscript.

July

4 (Thurs) Writes to Mrs Elliot concerning Ellen Ternan. (On the significance of this important but puzzling letter, see Slater, *Dickens and Women*, pp. 424–5.)

26 Layard visits Gad's Hill Place.

August

2   (Fri) Is suffering from a badly swollen left foot; by the 5th he is 'in tortures' (to JF, 6 Aug).

3   Dolby sails for America (see 13 June); in spite of his painful foot, CD goes to Liverpool to see him off.

23 Tells Wilkie Collins that he has written the opening chapter of *No Thoroughfare*, the Christmas story on which they are collaborating, and sends suggestions for the development of the plot.

September

2   (Mon) Tells Wills that he has received encouraging reports from Dolby. *The Times* publishes a letter from CD denying rumours that he is 'much out of health'.

3   Wilkie Collins and Reade are on a visit to Gad's Hill Place.

10 Tells Collins that he has been working 'steadily' but 'slowly' at *No Thoroughfare*. On the 23rd, he tells him that work is proceeding 'with snail-like slowness' and that he is distracted by thoughts of his forthcoming visit to America.

13 Tells Bulwer-Lytton that he has 'not yet decided' whether to visit America. (See also the 24th.)

17 Presides at a public meeting of the Printers' Readers' Association.

21 Dolby lands at Liverpool and proceeds straight to Gad's Hill; the next day, in the course of a walk to Cobham village and through Cobham Park, CD and Dolby discuss the possible visit to America.

24 Asks JF's and Wills's opinion whether he should go to America. After writing to Wills again on the 28th, and seeing JF, he sends a telegram to Boston on the 30th, stating definitely that he will go.

November

2   (Sat) CD's friends give a farewell banquet in his honour at the Freemasons' Hall, Bulwer-Lytton presiding. Nearly 450 guests are present, with more than 100 ladies watching from the gallery; CD is much moved by the occasion.

8   Travels to Liverpool.

9   CD sails for America in the *Cuba* under Captain Stone, after instructing Wills to forward to Ellen Ternan, who is in Florence,

a copy of the coded telegram that CD will send soon after his arrival (in the event the telegram tells her not to join him).

10 Arrives in Queenstown Harbour.
18 Arrives in Halifax, Nova Scotia.
19 Arrives in Boston, and is met by Dolby.
20 Receives a visit from Longfellow.
21 Dines at the home of J. T. Fields; the other guests include Longfellow, Emerson, Holmes and Agassiz.

December
1 (Sun) Visits the School Ship in Boston harbour, and gives a speech to the boys.
2 The American reading-tour opens in Boston with 'success . . . beyond description or exaggeration' (to Charley, 3 Dec). It comprises 75 readings and lasts until 20 April. There are other readings in Boston on the 3rd, 5th and 6th.
6 Tells Wills that the readings are making 'a *clear profit* of £1,300 per week!'
7 Travels to New York.
9 Gives his first reading in New York (others on the 10th, 12th, 13th, 16th, 17th, 19th and 20th). A week later he tells Bulwer-Lytton that his success in that city is 'beyond all precedent or description'.
21 Returns to Boston and (23rd–24th) gives two readings.
25 Returns to New York for seven more readings (26, 27, 28, 30 and 31 Dec; 2 and 3 Jan).
26 A dramatisation of *No Thoroughfare* by CD, Collins and Fechter opens in London.
27 The heavy cold from which CD has been suffering for several days is now so much worse that he sends for a doctor; the advice to cancel his readings for a few days is, however, resisted.

1868

January
3 (Fri) CD is still suffering from a heavy cold. At about this date he returns to Boston for readings on the 6th and 7th, but is back in New York by the 8th for readings there on the 9th and 10th.

12 Goes to Philadelphia for readings on the 13th and 14th.
15 Back in New York for four readings in Brooklyn (16th, 17th, 20th, 21st).
23–4 In Philadelphia again for two more readings; then to Baltimore for readings on the 27th and 28th; then in Philadelphia once more for a further two readings on the 30th and 31st.

February
1 (Sat) To Washington via Baltimore.
3 First reading in Washington, attended by the President and various members of the Cabinet. Further readings there on the 4th, 6th and 7th.
7 Visits President Andrew Johnson at the White House (it is CD's fifty-sixth birthday). He gives his final Washington reading; his cold is 'worse than ever' (to Georgina).
8 To Baltimore for readings (10th and 11th).
?12 To Philadelphia for his last two readings in that city (13th and 14th).
?15 To New York.
18 Reads at Hartford, Connecticut.
20 Reads in Providence, Rhode Island (and again on the 21st).
24 In Washington again.
25 In Boston for two weeks of readings. He reads there on the 24th, 25th, 27th and 28th; however, the impeachment ˙ of the President on the 24th precipitates a political crisis that empties the theatres, and by the 28th CD has decided to cancel the next week's readings (i.e. the second week planned in Boston). Since his persistent cold is no better, he welcomes the week's rest; however, he participates (with Dolby and Osgood) in a 'Great International Walking Match' on the 29th.

March
2 (Mon) to 6 Boston readings cancelled during this week (see previous entry).
4 Dines with Longfellow.
6 Spends the night at Albany.
7 Travels to Syracuse.
8 Tells Fechter that he is 'growing very homesick'.
9 Reads in Syracuse.
10 Reads in Rochester.

12   Reads in Buffalo (and again on the 13th); learns of the death of
     Chauncy Hare Townshend.
14   Goes to Niagara Falls for 'two most brilliant days' of sight-
     seeing (to JF, 16 Mar).
15   Returns to Rochester for another reading on the 16th.
17   Makes an early start for Albany (a railway journey of some
     eleven hours); on account of flooding, they are stranded at
     Utica and spend the night there, not reaching Albany until 3.30
     p.m. on the 18th. CD reads in Albany that evening, and gives
     another reading there the next day.
20   Reads in Springfield, Massachusetts.
23   Reads in Worcester, Massachusetts.
24   Reads in New Haven, Connecticut.
25   Reads in Hartford, Connecticut.
27   Is so exhausted that he cannot get up to catch the morning train
     for New Bedford; he takes a later train that gets him there just in
     time for the reading that evening.
28   Travels to Portland (Maine) via Boston.
29   Tells Mary Dickens that he has been 'absolutely sleepless' and
     has lost his appetite.
30   Reads in Portland.
31   Leaves Portland at 6 a.m. to return to Boston.

April
 1   (Wed) Gives the first of six farewell readings in Boston (others
     on the 2nd, 3rd, 6th, 7th and 8th).
 3   'Catarrh worse than ever!' (to Georgina).
13   Gives the first of five farewell readings in New York (others on
     the 14th, 16th, 17th and 20th).
18   Is entertained to a farewell dinner by the New York press,
     although he is in great pain from a swollen foot and cannot get
     the boot on.
20   Final reading of the American tour.
22   Leaves New York for Liverpool on the *Russia*, having made a
     net profit on the tour of about £19,000. Anthony Trollope, who
     is in America on Post Office business, turns up unexpectedly to
     see him off.
26   At sea, and already feeling 'greatly better' (to Fields).
30   The *Russia* arrives in Queenstown harbour at 4 a.m. after a 'very
     rough' Atlantic crossing (Dolby).

May

1   (Fri) Arrives in Liverpool, spending the night at the Adelphi Hotel.

2   Proceeds to London and thence to Gad's Hill Place, where he is given an enthusiastic welcome by the Higham villagers.

7   Dolby visits CD and finds him fully recovered from his exertions during the reading tour.

During this month, CD sees the dramatisation of *No Thoroughfare* at the Adelphi Theatre twice, and also makes a brief visit to Paris in order to advise on a French version of the play that is running there.

June

10   (Wed) Tells Macready that he is 'overwhelmed' with work (he is carrying an extra editorial burden in connection with *AYR* since Wills is unable to work as a result of concussion from a hunting-accident, and in addition his duties as literary executor for Townshend are proving very burdensome).

July

2   (Thurs) Attends, as godfather, the christening of Dolby's son.

4–6   Longfellow and members of his family spend the weekend at Gad's Hill Place. JF and Kent join the party for a day, and they all visit Rochester.

31   CD writes to Wills, apparently from Windsor Lodge, Peckham (home of Ellen Ternan).

August

18   (Tues) Two American visitors, Dr Fordyce Barker (who had attended CD in New York) and Bayard Taylor, dine at Gad's Hill Place.

September

26   (Sat) CD sees his youngest child, Edward, off for Australia – 'a sad parting . . . I have not been myself since' (to Wills, 27 Sep); 'I did not think I could have been so shaken' (to Fletcher); 'I find myself constantly thinking of Plorn [the boy's nickname]' (to Georgina, 11 Oct).

October

During this month, CD's son Henry (Harry) begins his studies at Trinity Hall, Cambridge.

 6 (Tues) CD opens his farewell series of (as it transpired) 72
    readings with a London reading at the St James's Hall;
    Chappell's will pay him £80 per performance.
10 Reads in the Free Trade Hall, Manchester.
11 To Liverpool for three readings (12th–14th).
17 Reads in Manchester again.
19 Reads in Brighton.
20 Death of Frederick Dickens, brother of CD. Reads in London.
22 Reads in Brighton again.
23 Travels to Manchester and reads there on the 24th.
25 In Liverpool; he tells JF, 'I have not been well, and have been
    heavily tired'. Reads there on 26th, 27th and 28th.
30 Tells Fields that he has 'serious thoughts of doing the murder
    from Oliver Twist; but it is so horrible, that I am going to try it on
    a dozen people in my London hall one night next month,
    privately, and see what effect it makes' (see 14 Nov). On 29
    September he had told Dolby, 'You shall look through the
    Murder as I have arranged it.'
31 Reads in Manchester.

November
On account of a general election, there are few readings during this
month.
 2 (Mon) Reads in Brighton.
 3 Reads in London.
 7 Reads in Brighton.
14 Reads *Sikes and Nancy* to an invited audience of about one
    hundred, including members of the press, at the St James's
    Hall. Afterwards, JF, Dolby and Charley Dickens all advise him
    not to read it in public; Wilkie Collins and Charles Kent,
    however, urge him to do so, but to expand the narrative to
    include the death of Sikes. (It is performed on 5 Jan 1869 and on
    27 other occasions during the final tour.)
17 Reads in London.

December
 1 (Tues) Reads in London.
 5 Travels to Edinburgh.
 6 CD and Dolby walk to Arthur's Seat.
 7 Reads in Edinburgh.
 8 'I am perpetually counting the weeks before me to be "read"

through, and am perpetually longing for the end of them; and yet I sometimes wonder whether I shall miss something when they are over' (to Wilkie Collins).

9   Reads in Glasgow.

11 Reads in Edinburgh, and again on the 14th.

15–18 In Glasgow for three readings (15th–17th), then to Edinburgh again for a matinée on the 19th.

22 Reads in London.

CD spends Christmas at Gad's Hill Place. On Boxing Day he reports himself to Dolby as 'Commencing a course of Oliver' – that is, rehearsing *Sikes and Nancy* for its first public performance on 5 January.

1869

January

1   (Fri) CD reports to F. D. Finlay that Georgina has been 'very unwell', but is now 'much better' and will accompany him on his forthcoming visit to Ireland.

5   First public reading of *Sikes and Nancy* (at the St James's Hall).

7   Accompanied by Georgina, Dolby and Fitzgerald, CD travels to Belfast, where he reads on the 8th and the 15th. He also reads in Dublin on the 11th, 12th and 13th.

17 Back in London. Reads there on the 19th.

20 Reads in Clifton.

21 Reads in Newport.

22 In Cheltenham, where (23rd) Macready attends, and is much impressed by, his reading of *Sikes and Nancy*.

24 Visits Dolby's home at Ross and walks with him from Ross to Monmouth.

25 Reads at Clifton.

27 Reads in Torquay.

29–30 In Bath for two readings.

February

2   (Tues) Reads in London. Visits Chorley.

4   Reads in Nottingham.

5   Reads in Leicester.

6–8 At Gad's Hill Place. Wilkie Collins and the Forsters join CD there on the 7th to celebrate his fifty-seventh birthday.

15   At his doctor's insistence, CD cancels a London reading on the
      16th and a planned journey to Edinburgh on the 17th, on
      account of 'inflammation of the foot (caused by over-exertion)'
      (medical statement).
20   Goes to Edinburgh to resume the postponed readings.
22   Reads in Glasgow.
24   Reads in Edinburgh.
25   Reads in Glasgow again.
26   Reads in Edinburgh again.
27   Returns to London.

March
2   (Tues) Reads in London.
4   Reads in Wolverhampton.
6   Reads in Manchester. He also spends Sunday the 7th there and
     drives to Alderley Edge.
8   Shortly before catching the train from Manchester to Hull, CD
     receives news of the death (on the 6th) of Sir James Emerson
     Tennent; Dolby finds him 'in a paroxysm of grief'. He proceeds
     to Hull and reads there on the 9th.
11   After a rest-day on the 10th, he reads in York. Immediately after
     the performance (from which the intervals have been omitted to
     enable him to catch his train), he dashes to the station and
     catches the 9.45 p.m. train to London in order to attend
     Tennent's funeral the next day.
16   Reads in London.
17   Reads in Ipswich.
18   Reads in Cambridge.
20   Reads in Manchester (and again on the 22nd).
29   Attends a performance of *Black and White*, by Wilkie Collins and
     Fechter, at the Adelphi Theatre.
30   Reads in London.
31   Resumes the provincial tour with a reading at Sheffield.

April
1   (Thurs) Reads in Birmingham (and again on the 2nd).
3   To Liverpool for four farewell readings (5th, 6th, 8th, 9th).
10   A civic banquet is given in CD's honour at St George's Hall,
     Liverpool.
13   Reads in London.
16   Reads in Leeds.

17–18 In Chester for a weekend's rest; while there he feels symptoms referred to below (see entries for 19th and 21st).

19 Reads in Blackburn. He writes to Dr Beard that he is 'extremely giddy, extremely uncertain of my footing (especially on the left side) and extremely indisposed to raise my hands to my head'. He enquires whether the medicine he is taking for 'an occasional return of that effusion of blood from piles' (to Beard, 13 Apr) could be responsible for these symptoms; but Beard later assures him that this cannot be the case.

20 Reads in Bolton.

21 In Blackpool for a day's rest. He writes to Georgina, 'My weakness and deadness are all *on the left side*, and if I don't look at anything I try to touch with my left hand, I don't know where it is'; he also tells Beard that the symptoms, though by now 'greatly moderated', are 'all *on the left side*'.

22 In Preston. Beard arrives from London, visits CD, and tells him that the readings must be stopped at once or he will not be answerable for the consequences to CD's health. As a result, the Preston reading and the rest of the tour are cancelled, 72 readings having been given out of a planned total of 100. (See 'A Fly-leaf in a Life', *UT*.)

23 Goes to London.

May

3 (Mon) Describes himself to Fitzgerald as 'in a brilliant condition'.

12 Makes a will that includes a legacy of £1000 to Ellen Ternan.

18 Dines with Fields, who is visiting England; afterwards they go 'with some of the Police, to have a glimpse of the darker side of London life' (to Sol Eytinge, 14 May) – specifically, the Ratcliffe Highway, where they see an old woman who later serves as a model for Princess Puffer in *ED*. They make another similar expedition on the 31st. During the Fields's visit to London, CD, Mary and Georgina stay at the St James's Hotel in Piccadilly.

24 Dines with Fields and his wife after taking them sight-seeing in London.

29 Visits Windsor and Richmond with the Fields; they dine at the Star and Garter, Richmond.

June

1 (Tues) Has finished an article 'On Mr Fechter's Acting' for the *Atlantic Monthly* (published in the August issue).

2 Fields and his wife, with Mabel Lowell and Eytinge, arrive at Gad's Hill Place for a week's visit. The large house-party also includes Dr Fordyce Barker, Dolby and Ouvry. They make various excursions, including (on the 7th) one to Canterbury via Rochester, Chatham, Sittingbourne and Faversham.

July
20 (Tues) CD reports himself to Macready as 'perfectly well and flourishing'; however, on 8 August he tells Mrs Elliot that he has had 'some distressing indications that I am not yet as well as I hoped I was'.
During this month he sends to JF 'the idea of a story' (see the next entry).

August
6 (Fri) Tells JF that he has 'laid aside the fancy I told you of', and now has 'a very curious and new idea for my new story' – the germ of *ED*.
20 Writes down seventeen possible titles for his new novel.
30 Speaks at a dinner of the London Rowing Club for the Oxford and Harvard crews at the Crystal Palace.

September
6 (Mon) Tells Arthur Ryland that among other business in hand is 'the title of a new book'.
24 Allows Charles Collins to 'try his hand' at illustrating his new novel by first attempting a cover-design.
27 Speaks at a meeting of the Birmingham and Midland Institute, of which he agreed (on 23 Jan) to serve as president for the academic year.

October
18 (Mon) Tells Macready that he is 'in the preliminary agonies' of his new novel. During this month he reads the opening chapters of *ED* to Fields.

November
4 (Thurs) Tells T. A. Trollope that the new book is 'just begun'.
28 On account of ill health, Charles Collins has given up the position of illustrator for ED after executing only the cover-design, which CD regards as 'excellent' (to JF, 22 Dec).

December

1   (Wed) The printer informs CD that the first two numbers of *ED*
     are altogether '*twelve printed pages too short!!!*' (to JF, 22 Dec), and
     the next two or three weeks are spent in making good this
     deficiency as well as rehearsing the readings.

22   The first two numbers of *ED* are 'now in type' (to JF).
     Christmas is spent at Gad's Hill Place. On Boxing Day, a sports
     meeting takes place in the field adjoining Gad's Hill Place (*cf.* 26 Dec
     1866), and CD makes a speech to the assembled company.

1870

January

During this month, CD rents 5 Hyde Park Place until June, 'on
Mary's account' (to Mrs Elliot, 28 Dec 1869). Mary is still (and is to
remain) unmarried and there are presumably still hopes that she
may find a husband during the London season.

6   (Thurs) CD distributes the prizes at the Birmingham and
     Midland Institute prize-giving held in Birmingham Town Hall.

11   Begins his final series of twelve London readings at the St
     James's Hall. They continue to 15 March, at well-spaced
     intervals. There is a matinée reading on the 14th and another on
     the 21st, and evening readings on the 18th and 25th. According
     to Dolby, CD's 'feverish excitement and bodily pain' increase
     during this series of readings; Dolby also records that during
     performances CD's pulse-rate rises from 72 to as high as 124.

February

The London series of readings continues during this month, with
performances on the 1st, 8th, 15th and 22nd. Work on *ED* also
continues.

12   Death of George Hogarth, father-in-law of CD.

March

Readings are given on the 1st, 8th and 15th.

2   (Wed) Tells Macready that work on *ED* is going 'very well'.

3   Dines with Wills.

6   Goes to lunch at George Eliot's home; Lewes is also present.

9   CD has an audience with Queen Victoria at Buckingham Palace,
     having signified his willingness on the 3rd and being

introduced by Arthur Helps, Clerk of the Privy Council. On the 26th, having meanwhile attended a levée, he sends her an advance copy of the first number of *ED* and offers to 'anticipate the publication' if she 'should ever be sufficiently interested in the tale to desire to know a little more of it in advance of her subjects' (she does not seem to have taken up the offer). At the audience on the 9th, the Queen finds him, according to her journal, 'very agreeable, with a pleasant voice and manner'.

15 Concludes the series of London readings, and his career as a reader in public, with a performance of the *Carol* and the Trial from *Pickwick* – his 472nd public reading, according to Philip Collins's computation.

April

1   (Fri) Serialisation of *ED* begins; the new novel is warmly welcomed by reviewers after CD's unprecedented silence as a novelist for nearly five years.

5   Presides at the annual dinner of the Newsvendors' Benevolent Institution.

6   Attends a levée given by the Prince of Wales.

7   Gives a reception and supper; the guests include many notabilities in the literary, artistic and fashionable worlds, and music is provided by some of the leading performers of the day.

18 Tells Fields that the first number of *ED* has been 'doing wonders' and has *'very, very far outstripped every one of its predecessors'* in point of sales. (Sales of the opening number reach 50,000.)

25 Tells Kent that during the previous week he has been 'most perseveringly and ding-dong-doggedly at work' on *ED*, but has been 'making headway but slowly'.

27 Hears of the death of Maclise two days earlier.

30 Speaks at the Royal Academy banquet.

May

Early in the month, CD attends a breakfast given by the Prime Minister, Mr Gladstone.

11 (Wed) Is suffering from 'a neuralgic affection of the foot' (to Mrs E. M. Ward), and cancels a dinner engagement for the 12th, also a dinner for the General Theatrical Fund and all other dinner engagements (including one with JF) for the following week. However, he keeps many other social engagements during this

month, including dinner at Lord Stanhope's and at Dean Stanley's and a visit to the theatre with Lady Molesworth.

22 Last meeting with JF.

23 Death of Mark Lemon. CD attempts to obtain a pension for Lemon's family through the Prime Minister.

June

3 (Fri) Returns to Gad's Hill Place from London.

5 CD's daughter Kate, who has arrived the previous day, finds him looking 'a good deal changed'; he tells her that he hopes *ED* will prove a success 'if, please God, I live to finish it', and that he has 'not been strong lately'. He is 'cheerful and talkative' at dinner, but a short walk in the garden leaves him 'fatigued'. (Kate's accounts of this visit are conveniently excerpted in Collins, *Dickens: Interviews and Recollections*, pp. 354–7.)

8 Still at Gad's Hill Place, CD plans to visit London the next day to meet Wills and to deal with *AYR* business. He works on the manuscript of *ED*; at dinner ('between 6 and 7 o'clock', according to *The Times* for 10 June), he suffers a stroke and never regains consciousness.

9 CD dies at 6.10 p.m. Mary, Kate, Charley, Dr Beard and Ellen Ternan are among those in the house at the time.

10 Millais makes a sketch of CD's head and Woolner a death mask.

14 His body is conveyed by special train from Gad's Hill Place to Charing Cross Station, and thence by hearse, for a private funeral at Westminster Abbey. The mourners include his two daughters, his sons Charles and Henry, Georgina Hogarth, JF, Beard and Wilkie Collins.

19 Dean Stanley preaches the sermon at a public funeral service held in Westminster Abbey.

September

1 (Thurs) Publication of the sixth and last instalment of *ED* and of the novel in volume form.

CD left about £93,000. JF and Georgina Hogarth were his executor and executrix, and JF became his authorised biographer, his *Life* appearing in 1872–4. JF himself died in 1876 and left his collection of CD's manuscripts and other material to what is now the Victoria and Albert Museum (Forster Collection).

Catherine Dickens outlived her husband, dying in 1879. Of their eight children who survived CD, Sydney died at sea in 1872; Francis died in America in 1886; Charley died in 1896, after publishing various reminiscences of his father; Mary, who had remained a devoted unmarried daughter, also died in 1896 (at exactly the same age, as Michael Slater points out, as her father); Edward died in Australia in 1902; Alfred died in America in 1912; Kate, who had remarried in 1874, died in 1929 after communicating her memories to Gladys Storey, whose *Dickens and Daughter* was published in 1939; and Henry, who became a Queen's Counsel, received a knighthood, and published reminiscences of his father, died in 1933.

Georgina Hogarth lived until 1916. With Mary (Mamie) Dickens, she published in 1880–2 the first major collection of CD's letters. Mamie also published *My Father as I Recall Him* (1897) and other reminiscences. CD was survived by one of his sisters, Letitia, who died in 1874. Ellen Ternan married a clergyman and schoolmaster in 1876 and died in 1914; her relationship with CD did not come to light until twenty years after her death.

Sources

My most important source has been Dickens's own letters – to the end of 1849, in the five volumes that have so far appeared (from 1965) in the magnificent Pilgrim Edition under the general editorship of Madeline House, Graham Storey and (latterly) Kathleen Tillotson; and thereafter in the much less satisfactory but still useful Nonesuch Edition edited by Walter Dexter (3 vols, 1938). Apart from the letters themselves, the admirable annotations of the Pilgrim Edition have been enormously helpful. For Dickens's speeches, I have used *The Speeches of Charles Dickens*, ed. K. J. Fielding (1960), supplemented by Philip Collins, 'Some Uncollected Speeches by Dickens', *Dickensian*, 73 (1977) 89–99. For Dickens's readings, Professor Collins's *Charles Dickens: The Public Readings* (1975) has been indispensable; additional information has also been drawn from George Dolby's *Charles Dickens as I Knew Him* (1885). Among the numerous biographies of Dickens, the most useful have been (not unexpectedly) John Forster's *The Life of Charles Dickens* (1872–4) and Edgar Johnson's *Charles Dickens: His Tragedy and Triumph* (1952). The notes in J. W. T. Ley's edition of Forster's work (1928) have yielded further information, as have Robert Langton's *The Childhood and Youth of Charles Dickens* (1891) and Thomas Wright's *The Life of Charles Dickens* (1935). For reliable information concerning the publication of Dickens's work and his relationships with his publishers, Robert L. Patten's *Charles Dickens and his Publishers* (1978) has been very valuable; further details concerning some of the novels have been provided by those volumes that have so far appeared in the Clarendon Edition.

The back numbers of *The Dickensian* over the last eighty years have supplied many details too numerous and widely scattered to be here acknowledged separately; but particular mention should be made of the fresh light thrown on Dickens's early years by Angus Easson's essay 'John Dickens and the Navy Pay Office' (70 [1974] 34–45) and by a series of articles by Michael Allen: 'The Dickens Family at Portsmouth, 1807–14' (77 [1981] 131–43); 'The Dickens Family at London and Sheerness, 1815–1817' (78 [1982] 3–7); 'The Dickens Family at Chatham, 1817–1822' (78 [1982] 67–87); 'The Dickens Family in London, 1822–1824' (78 [1982] 131–51); and 'The Dickens Family in London, 1824–1827' (79 [1983] 3–20).

For information on Dickens's contemporaries, the following have been consulted:

Adrian, Arthur A., *Georgina Hogarth and the Dickens Circle* (1957).
——, *Mark Lemon: First Editor of 'Punch'* (1966).
Aylmer, Felix, *Dickens Incognito* (1959).
Bredsdorff, Elias, *Hans Christian Andersen* (1975).
Collins, Philip (ed.), *Dickens: Interviews and Recollections* (1981).
Davies, James A., *John Forster: A Literary Life* (1983).
Eliot, George, *Letters*, ed. G. S. Haight (1954–6).
Fielding, K. J., 'Charles Dickens and his Wife: Fact or Forgery?', *Etudes Anglaises*, 8 (1955) 212–22.
Gérin, Winifred, *Elizabeth Gaskell: A Biography* (1976).
Macready, W. C., *The Diaries of William Charles Macready 1833–1851*, ed. William Toynbee (1912).
Martin, Robert Bernard, *Tennyson: The Unquiet Heart* (1980).
Nisbet, Ada, *Dickens and Ellen Ternan* (1952).
Ray, G. N., *Thackeray: The Uses of Adversity* (1955).
——, *Thackeray: The Age of Wisdom* (1958).
Robinson, Kenneth, *Wilkie Collins: A Biography* (1974).
Sadleir, Michael, *Blessington–D'Orsay: A Masquerade* (1933).
——, *Bulwer and his Wife: A Panorama* (1931).
Slater, Michael, *Dickens and Women* (1983).
Storey, Gladys, *Dickens and Daughter* (1939).
Super, R. H., *Walter Savage Landor: A Biography* (1957).
Thackeray, W. M., *Letters and Private Papers*, ed. G. N. Ray (1945–6).
Yates, Edmund, *His Recollections and Experiences* (1885).

For minor figures the *Dictionary of National Biography* has, as usual, been indispensable. The files of *The Times* have been consulted, mainly for their accounts of the death and burial of Dickens and others.

Index

This index is divided into three sections:
(1) The writings of Charles Dickens;
(2) People;
(3) Places: (a) London; (b) British Isles (outside London); (c) Europe; (d) North America.

1 THE WRITINGS OF CHARLES DICKENS

2 PEOPLE

Agassiz, Jean Louis (1807–73), 128
Ainsworth, William Harrison
(1805–82), novelist, 11, 13, 15,
17, 25, 26, 34, 38, 41, 43, 61, 62
Albert, Prince (1819–61), Prince
Consort, 21, 22, 47, 63, 75, 95,
110
Alexander, Francis (1800–?81),
American portrait-painter, 30
Alison, Sir Archibald (1792–1867),
lawyer and historian, 60
Alison, Dr William (1790–1859),
medical professor, 27
Allan, Sir William (1782–1850),
historical painter, 22, 27
Allen, Mrs Mary, née Barrow, later
Mrs Matthew Lamert, aunt of
CD (d. 1822), 3
Andersen, Hans (1805–75), Danish
author, 58–9, 93, 94–5
Austin, Henry (?1812–61), architect
and civil engineer, brother-in-
law of CD, 12, 37, 66, 109

Ballantine, William (1812–87),
serjeant-at-law, 14
Barham, Richard Harris (1788–
1845), clergyman and poet, 17,
34, 41, 45
Barker, Dr Fordyce, American
physician, 131, 136
Barrow, Charles (1759–1826),
grandfather of CD, 1
Barrow, John Henry (1796–1858),
uncle of CD, 6

Beadnell, Anne (Mrs H. Kolle)
(d.1836), 7, 10
Beadnell, George (1773–1862),
bank clerk, 6, 112
Beadnell, Maria (Mrs Henry
Winter) (1810–86), daughter of
George Beadnell, 6, 7, 87–8, 112
Beard, Francis (Frank) (1814–93),
physician, 107, 119–20, 135, 139
Beard, Thomas (1807–91),
journalist, 7, 8, 11, 14, 17, 19, 21,
43, 61, 68, 76, 79, 84, 86, 88, 93,
94, 105, 111, 113, 126
Bentley, Richard (1794–1871),
publisher 10, 11, 13, 15, 17, 20,
21, 22
Black, John (1782–1855), editor, 8
Blackwood, Alexander (1805–43),
publisher, 27
Blackwood, Robert (1807–52),
publisher, 27
Blanchard, Samuel Laman (1804–
45), author, 7, 17, 20, 21, 38, 45, 46
Blanchard, Sidney Laman (?1827–
83), journalist, son of Samuel
Laman Blanchard, 47
Blessington, Countess of (1789–
1849), hostess and authoress, 21,
26, 35, 40, 42, 47, 49, 50, 55, 67
Boyle, the Hon. Mary (1810–90),
69, 72, 78, 92, 105, 109
Bradbury & Evans, printers, 47, 49,
50, 53, 66, 76, 103; *see also*
William Bradbury, Frederick M.
Evans

3 PLACES